INTRODUC... NORSE MYTHOLOGY FOR KIDS

INTRODUCTION TO NORSE MYTHOLOGY FOR KIDS

A FUN COLLECTION OF THE GREATEST HEROES, MONSTERS, AND GODS IN NORSE MYTH

PETER APERLO

ULYSSES PRESS

Published in the United States by:
Ulysses Press
PO Box 3440
Berkeley, CA 94703
www.ulyssespress.com

ISBN: 978-1-64604-190-9
Library of Congress Control Number: 2021931505

Printed in the United States by Kingery Printing Company
10 9 8 7 6 5 4 3 2 1

Acquisitions editor: Casie Vogel
Managing editor: Claire Chun
Project manager: Bridget Thoreson
Proofreader: Renee Rutledge
Front cover design: Jake Flaherty
Cover images: from shutterstock.com Thor © delcarmat; Valkyrie
      © GoodStudio; knot graphic © Hoika Mikhail
Interior illustrations: Valentin Ramon

For Professor Jesse Byock,
who has forgotten more about the Vikings
than any of us will ever know.

And for Lee Fair,
who taught me the most important question
in the study of history is "why?"

CONTENTS

INTR✛DUCTI✛N

Call them Vikings or call them Norsemen, chances are you've seen plenty of these guys in pop culture over the years. Movies, TV, books, and comics are filled with the thrilling and often bloody adventures of these shaggy, seagoing barbarians. And with them come amazing stories of heroes, gods, and monsters.

You've probably already heard some of their names, such as Odin, Thor, Loki, and the Midgard Serpent. Others may be new to you—like Bodvar Bjarki. In this book you'll read stories that are comical as well as gruesome, some that are incredibly noble, and others that are simply mystifying.

From the creation of the world to the final battle of Ragnarok between the gods and the forces of evil, these are stories that are crucial to know if you want to fully understand the world of the Vikings.

Where Did These Stories Come From?

A thousand years ago, the Vikings and other people of northern Europe—the region we now know as Scandinavia—recorded vibrant sagas and poems. They collected an impressive array of stories revolving around ancient myths and beliefs—and amazingly, these were preserved at a time when many ancient tales were lost as the region converted to Christianity.

The Vikings themselves are often seen as lawless terrors and masters of hit-and-run tactics that made them the scourge of an entire continent. Looting, burning, and killing seemed to be their main pastimes, carried out with savage zeal. But what if that wasn't the whole story?

This book dispels some of the misconceptions about these fascinating people. We'll show how their culture was every bit as sophisticated as the so-called civilized peoples around them—and even more sophisticated in terms of the people's voice in government, and sometimes even women's rights. We'll explain how the Vikings built powerful kingdoms that challenged their neighbors on an equal footing. You'll see how, in the midst of the Dark Ages, when most Europeans never left their villages, these adventurous Scandinavians explored and traded all the way from Asia across to North America.

Some elements may remind you of other traditions you're familiar with—Greek, Roman, and Celtic, for example. But I think you'll agree that the Norse myths have a certain energy and vitality that set them apart. These stories hold a unique place in our shared cultural heritage and are worth dusting off—whether you're becoming reacquainted with them or just now discovering them for the first time.

Onward!

VIKING CULTURE

Who Were the Vikings, Really?

There was never an ethnic group called the Vikings. If you try to look up Vikingland on any map, ancient or modern, you won't find it. No one ever spoke Vikingish. Who, then, are these Vikings we see so often in books, cartoons, and movies?

The word "Viking" comes directly from Old Norse—the language they *did* speak. "Vik" means a small bay or inlet, while "ing" means "a person." This "Bay-Person" was a pirate and a raider, someone who roved the seas in search of goods to plunder. Viking targets included monasteries filled with priceless gold and silver ornaments and relics; farmsteads rich with cattle, food, and even people to sell as slaves; and well-defended, walled towns ripe to be sacked. Sometimes the Vikings actually traded goods (ill-gotten or not) with the folks they encountered, rather than fight them. Some of the things they did were pretty horrid, and we would find them unacceptable today.

Vikings set out on a raid

Vik: bay or inlet

So, being a Viking was a job, not a nationality. For some it was a full-time lifestyle, while for others it was temporary, a grand adventure. Sagas are full of young men getting hold of a ship or two and leaving their farms in spring and summer for a Viking expedition. (You didn't even have to come from Scandinavia to do this. There are chronicles that tell of Danish people complaining about Vikings harassing ships in the Baltic Sea— Vikings who would have been Slavs from central Europe!)

The vast majority of the folks in northern Europe while all this was going on weren't Vikings at all; they were farmers, artisans, tradesmen, wives, and fathers just trying to get by—usually without slaying their neighbors. Saddling all the Scandinavians of this time with the term "Viking" would be a bit like somebody a thousand years from now referring to all Americans as the Cowboys or the Stockbrokers. Still, the Vikings were the most famous of the Scandinavians, and it was their sudden burst of far-flung raiding and trading that gives us the term "Viking Age."

Exactly when the Viking Age occurred is open to debate, depending on your historical point of view. If you were on the pointy end of Viking violence, like the English, you'd probably say it started in AD 793 with a raid on the monastery at Lindisfarne, and it ended with the last invasion by a Norwegian king in 1066. (This is *not* the famous invasion by William the Conqueror that you might have read about, although William was a descendant of Scandinavian Vikings!) From the Danish point of view, on the other hand, you might look at the Viking Age from a commercial standpoint, starting with the founding of the first market towns around 750 and ending with the destruction of a major one of those towns in 1050 by a Norwegian king. (Yes, the same one who attacked England in 1066—more on him later.) But essentially, if you found yourself in Europe roughly between the years 800 and 1100, you'd be in the midst of the Viking Age and probably should learn to defend yourself.

Historians over the centuries have made much of the brutal nature of the Vikings and the horrific acts they committed. For example, there are the accounts of Vikings executing hated enemies by cutting the "Blood Eagle" on their backs and pulling out their lungs to form a pair of gory wings. If the victim didn't swiftly pass out from shock, he would soon die from suffocation. Another saga recounts a king-slayer having his intestines fastened to a tree and being forced to walk around it until he died—an excruciating process that could take hours.

Did these grisly killings actually happen? It's hard to say, since in many cases they weren't written down until hundreds of years after the supposed fact. Certainly, though, such stories aren't that much worse than tales about execution and torture methods in the more "civilized" parts of Europe at the time. Charlemagne, king of the Franks from 768 to 814, was fond of offering conquered pagans the choice of converting to Christianity or having their heads removed. He infamously slaughtered some 4,500 rebel Saxons at Verden (Germany) in 782. In Anglo-Saxon England, trial by ordeal was considered a perfectly satisfactory way of deciding guilt or innocence. People accused of a crime could be made to walk over hot coals or the sharp blade of a plowshare, or to stick an arm into boiling water. If the wounds healed after three days, it was taken as a sign from God that they should go free. Beating, blinding, amputation, and mutilation were considered acceptable punishment for a variety of crimes. These were, after all, the Dark Ages.

If the Vikings weren't so bad, relatively speaking, what was it that set them apart and struck such terror in the hearts of their victims? For one thing, early on they were able to take everyone by surprise. Here was a deadly force that seemed to be able to strike anywhere, at any time. When Vikings sacked the isolated island monastery at Lindisfarne off the northeast coast of England, it was as if they had appeared out of thin air. People were shocked and outraged, but mostly frightened out of their wits.

How could the Vikings launch such devastating attacks without warning? The reason was their mastery of open-water sailing ships, which made them incredibly mobile. We'll talk about Viking ships later (see How Did People Get Around? on page 31), but suffice it to say that for the average peasant used to small fleets hugging the coast or armies plodding noisily along the muddy roads—pretty much announcing their arrival well in advance—the thought of armed foreigners who could suddenly show up wherever they liked was enough to make them soil their woolen trousers.

The other thing that made the Vikings so frightening was the fact that they were different: they were pagans. Most of Europe had converted to Christianity by this time (some parts quite recently), and imaginations ran wild with thoughts of what these barbarians with their heathen rites might do to them. The Blood Eagle torture, for example, was said to be a sacrifice to the god Odin. Who wants to become a human sacrifice? (Quick answer: Nobody!) And certainly Vikings had shown zero respect for Christian holy sites when they assaulted, looted, and burned monasteries over and over again. (Of course, that's where they found undefended treasures. What was to be expected?) The idea that pagans could turn up, slaughter a bunch of monks, make off with boatloads of holy relics, and not be immediately punished by God—well, that shook people to the core. Some saw the Vikings as divine retribution for the sins of the world. For others, the attacks simply signaled that the noblemen and military leaders who had promised to protect them were powerless to do so. The coming of the Vikings meant that things were going to change.

THINGS TO TAKE AWAY:

- "Viking" was an occupation, not an ethnic group.

- Only a small percentage of the people in Scandinavia during the Viking Age were actually Vikings.

- The Vikings were terrifying because they seemed to be able to attack almost anywhere without warning, and because they were seen as barbaric heathens.

What Were Their Homelands Like?

Though they shared a common language— which they called the "Danish tongue" and we call Old Norse—the peoples of Scandinavia during the Viking Age inhabited surprisingly diverse environments. Some lived on lowland farmsteads and supplemented what they could grow by fishing, while others trapped animals for their fur and logged the dense pine forests. Still others made their living as skilled craftsmen in the newly forming market towns.

A Viking-era map of Scandinavia would have looked a little different from today's countries of Denmark, Norway, and Sweden. Here we'll look at the most important areas to know about, from the Viking point of view.

VIKING VOCAB

Danish tongue: Old Norse, the language of Viking Age Scandinavia

■■

Denmark

In Viking times, Denmark consisted of not only the Jutland Peninsula and dozens of islands in the Baltic Sea (the largest being Fyn and Sjaelland), but also the southern portion of what is now Sweden. Made up almost entirely of plains and low, rolling hills—the highest point less than 600 feet above sea level— Denmark had the best farmland in all of Scandinavia along with moderate rainfall, warm summers, and relatively mild winters. Besides fishing in the surrounding seas, the Danes could grow a variety of crops (such as rye, barley, peas, beans, and cabbage) and raise many types of livestock (including sheep, pigs, goats, and cattle). As a result, Denmark could support the biggest population of any of the Scandinavian regions.

Straddling the North Sea and the Baltic Sea, Denmark was also uniquely situated to control trade flowing in both directions—slaves and silver coming from the east, and glass, wine, and weapons from the west. In the eighth century, Ribe and Hedeby were the first towns to spring up at the base of the Jutland Peninsula as a result of this commercial activity.

Norway

Norway was glued together by a trade route, too, but this one went in a north-south direction. In fact, the country's name means "north way" in Old Norse. In spite of having relatively mild weather, there was little quality farmland due to the mountainous nature of much of the country (the mountain range known as "The Keel" was mostly uninhabitable) and only a short growing season because of the long winters. Farming mostly meant raising goats and sheep. What Norway did have, however, was an abundance of fjords—narrow waterways flowing in from the sea between icy cliffs—and a series of offshore islands. Known as the Skerry Guard, these islands provided a sort of sheltered, ice-free highway for ships traveling up and down the coast. In addition to providing excellent fishing grounds, this allowed the Norwegians to journey far into the Arctic region

LAPPS

Hålogaland

Sea of Norway

The Keel mountain range

Trondheim

FINNS

NORWEGIANS

Sigtuna • Uppsala

Birka

Oslofjord

SVEAR

GOTAR

Skagerrak

Kattegat

North
Sea

Jutland

DANES

Jelling

Sjaelland

Baltic
Sea

SLAVS

Ribe •

Fyn

Hleidargard

Hedeby

Viking Age Scandinavia

known as Hålogaland to hunt and trade for furs and timber, as well as exotic goods such as falcons, narwhal horns, and walrus tusks.

Norway's two main population centers were the area around Trondheim in the north and the Oslofjord region in the south, both of which were agricultural and trading centers. Throughout the Viking Age, the leaders of these two regions would bump heads for control of the country—with the folks in between (where some of the most notorious Vikings came from) just trying to hang on to their independence.

Sweden

Sweden was actually home to two distinct peoples during the Viking period: the Svear and the Gotar. The Svear were concentrated in the rich farmland in the Lake Mälaren region, which was still connected to the Baltic Sea at that time and contained the major trading settlements of Birka and Sigtuna (near today's city of Stockholm). The Gotar were situated to the southwest near Lake Vänern, separated from the Svear by the Southern Uplands and the boggy area around Lake Vättern.

Sweden suffered more intense cold during the winter than Norway, with sea ice blocking access to the Baltic at times. The Svear especially looked eastward, raiding and trading in Slavic and Finnish lands for slaves, furs, amber, and Arabic silver. Due to their relative isolation, the Swedes were the last of the Scandinavians to convert to Christianity.

What Connected Everyone?

Something you might have figured out by looking at the map and reading a little about the geography is that traveling overland wasn't easy for the peoples of Scandinavia, due to the mountainous terrain and often marshy ground. The one thing that kept them all tied together, in spite of being so spread out across such varied locales, was a tradition of seafaring that went all the way back to the Stone Age. We'll take a look at their incredible ships and sea-based technology in the section How Did People Get Around? (page 31).

THINGS TO TAKE AWAY:

- Viking Age Scandinavians lived in diverse environments.

- Geography accounted for what kinds of food they could produce, where and what they traded, and how they got around.

What Did Norse People Look Like?

From images on stones and tapestries, descriptions in ancient literature, and cloth found in graves and at market towns, we have a pretty good idea of what people looked like during the Viking Age. Some things may surprise you.

Women typically wore a long-sleeved linen dress that reached to the ankles. Over this they wore a shorter, sleeveless pinafore-type dress made of wool, its straps fastened with oval brooches of bronze or even gold. Sleeves and hems were decorated with embroidery, sometimes in gold thread. Ankle-high shoes of supple leather completed the outfit, and a fine chain dangling from another brooch held essential tools: shears, knife, keys, and needle case. (Some women were even buried with these domestic tools.) When a woman ventured outside, she added a shawl or a woolen cape.

If a woman was married, she gathered her hair in a tight bun at the back of her neck and covered it with a close-fitting cap or scarf. Unmarried women wore their hair loose, or secured with a headband.

The standard look for men was a long-sleeved tunic of thick wool, fitted at the waist and reaching to mid-thigh, worn over a long linen shirt. Sometimes the tunic was belted, but often it hung loose. Men wore long trousers of two types: tight all the way down, or wide and baggy but gathered at the knee. Either sort might be secured on the lower leg by cross-garters or tucked into knee boots. Low, soft shoes were popular, too. Woolen and leather caps—pointed or rounded on top—offered protection from the cold northern winds. An embroidered silk ribbon—called a *hlad*—was worn as a headband for special occasions. Finishing the look was a long cape or cloak, sometimes draped over one shoulder to leave the sword arm free.

Norsemen cared about their appearance. They bathed and changed their clothes regularly, and they carried tweezers to prune facial hair, "ear spoons" to remove earwax, and combs to keep their hair, mustaches, and beards (all of which they sometimes bleached) groomed and free of lice. At one time, Danish fashion was to cut the hair short in back and leave the bangs

Men's and women's fashions of the Viking Age

longer—a sort of reverse mullet. Anglo-Saxons in England accused Norsemen of gussying up in order to lure away their women, though some Arabs were far less impressed with the Norsemen they encountered; one of them said they were "the filthiest of Allah's creatures."

Both men and women wore jewelry if they could get it. In addition to brooches, women favored necklaces, bracelets, and rings of gold and silver, often inlaid with precious stones, amber, or even colored glass. Men wore braided or twisted armbands of gold or silver, given as a reward for service to a king or jarl—a nobleman (earl) next down from the king in rank. Both men and women also used kohl eye makeup, a form of lead sulfide. Al-Tartushi, a traveler to Hedeby from Muslim Spain in the late-tenth century, remarked that when they apply this makeup, "their beauty never fades, but increases in both man and woman."

And you can forget that image of the huge, hulking Viking. Although undoubtedly muscular from living strenuous lives, most Scandinavians at this time were three to four inches shorter than modern-day Europeans due to poorer nutrition.

VIKING VOCAB

Hlad: Embroidered silk headband

Jarl: Nobleman just below a king in rank

Kohl: Form of lead sulfide used as eye makeup

■ ■

- Wool was a mainstay of the Norse people's wardrobes.

- Both men and women wore jewelry and makeup.

- Viking-era Scandinavians were shorter than we are.

What Was Life Like at Home?

Viking life wasn't all sailing, killing, and plundering (which, remember, most people in Scandinavia weren't doing at all). They had homes and families, whether on a farm or in one of the few towns. They ate, slept, worked, and amused themselves, just like we do—only different.

Halls and Houses

The vast majority of people in Scandinavia at this time lived a rural lifestyle on isolated farmsteads and in small villages. Their world revolved around the longhouse. Based on a tradition going back thousands of years, this structure was designed and oriented to slice through the prevailing winds and could be upwards of 100 feet long—about three to four times as long as it was wide. Most longhouses consisted of a single hall (*skali*) that served as bedroom, living room, kitchen, workshop, and even barn. (Living with the livestock was common throughout Europe at this time.)

Skali: Main hall of a longhouse

■ ■

The master and lady of the house often had a bedroom they could lock from the inside, but everyone else had to get on with their private lives as best they could out in the open, sleeping on benches that lined the walls. A central hearth and scattered braziers provided light and heat, making the window-less longhouses smoky much of the time.

Construction varied quite a bit, depending on what local materials were available. In Denmark, longhouses were normally built of plaster over wattle and daub (clay applied to a wicker frame), with thatched roofs. In timber-rich Norway and Sweden, the walls could be made of upright planks. In virtually treeless Iceland and Greenland—colonized mainly by settlers from Norway—homes had to be built from stones and blocks cut from the grassy turf, with walls that were sometimes 10 feet thick.

Smaller houses lined the unpaved streets of the trading towns. These were usually less than 50 feet long and about half that in width. Even smaller buildings were used for storage, and also for crafting and living quarters for some. Often the floors were dug out of the ground to provide insulation for the goods and people inside.

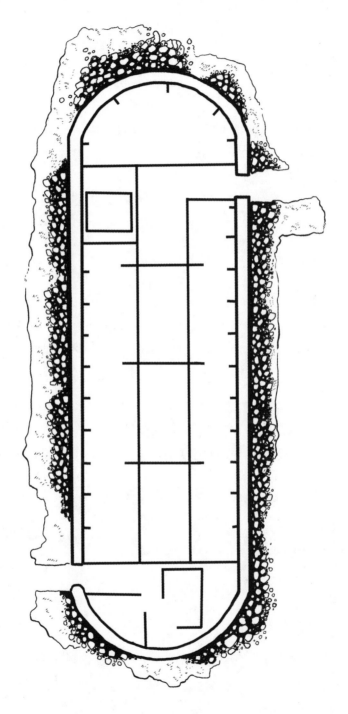

Plan of a longhouse

food

Whole-grain rye bread and porridge made of barley and oats were major staples of the Scandinavian diet. Of course, there was plenty of fish—especially herring. Beef, mutton, goat, pig, horse, and ox meat were usually boiled rather than roasted. Wild birds and small game could also be found on the menu, and seal, whale, and polar bear meat were popular in Norway, Iceland, and Greenland. The Scandinavians also consumed a variety of dairy products—milk and cheeses from the cows, sheep, and goats they raised.

Despite this seeming abundance, one bad harvest or a particularly long winter could threaten them with starvation. Preserving food was a real necessity, and people made extensive use of drying, fermenting, salting, smoking, and cooling with ice.

Table settings of the time included plates, spoons, and knives, but not yet forks. Drinking horns—usually made from the horns of domestic cattle—were typically filled with barley beer or with mead, a drink made from fermented honey and water. A strong fruit wine known as *bjorr* was also drunk.

VIKING VOCAB

Bjorr: Strong fruit wine

Mead: Fermented honey and water

Entertainment

The Norse people passed their free time in some of the same ways we do today. They enjoyed dice and board games—especially chess, checkers, and a local invention called *hnefatafl*, which pitted a king and his followers against a larger army of gaming pieces. People attended and bet on sporting events, such as *knattleikr*, a form of field hockey played with a hard ball and wooden bats. Men also wrestled, swam, and drank competitively. In Iceland, fights were staged between horses.

VIKING VOCAB

Hnefatafl: Board game

Knattleikr: Form of field hockey

These sports were all rougher than what would be allowed today, often resulting in serious injury and sometimes even in death. At the same time, Viking Age Scandinavians were folks who greatly appreciated poetry, and they enjoyed music played on horns, lyres, and flutes.

Family Life and Daily Work

The family unit living on a farmstead could be quite large. Besides immediate offspring, it might include extended relations, foster children, and a slave ("thrall") or two. A man was usually the head of the household, and he needed to be a jack-of-all-trades, whether he was a tenant or a landowner (unless he was one of the few specialized craftsmen). If he farmed, he also fished and hunted; if he was primarily a fisherman, he also plowed a plot of land. Every man traded goods to get the things his farm didn't produce. Every man also needed to be equipped and trained to fight, to defend his home or to answer the call to war from his king or jarl.

VIKING VOCAB

Thrall: Slave

▪▪▪▪▪▪▪▪▪▪▪▪▪▪▪▪▪▪▪▪▪▪▪▪▪▪▪▪▪▪▪▪▪▪▪▪▪▪ ▪ ▪

A woman's work, on the other hand, kept her close to home. She was responsible for spinning and weaving the wool, milking the livestock, churning the butter, grinding the grain, cooking the meals, and raising the children. This is not to say that she was treated as a servant—on the contrary, a freeborn Norse woman had more rights than most women in Europe at that time. She had a big say in how the household was run from day to day, and this was absolute if her husband was away or she was a widow.

A wife could divorce her husband if she felt the marriage wasn't working out, and her dowry and bride price (the latter paid by her husband to her father) were hers to take with her. Women also accompanied their men on some of their voyages of conquest and settlement. In the sagas, women are often the first to speak up, shaming their men into fighting to defend the family honor.

Most children didn't go to school at all. (Exceptions were those who chose a life in the church as a priest or a monk.)

Life inside a Viking Age longhouse

They learned all they needed to know from watching and helping their parents with chores around the house. Some parents even taught their children to read, using either Latin letters or runes or both (see Runes page 37). Boys generally followed in their fathers' footsteps in whatever trade they labored at, while girls learned how to run a household from their mothers.

THINGS TO TAKE AWAY:

- Most folks lived in one-room longhouses, along with their animals.

- They ate a simple diet of bread and porridge, along with meat and fish (when they could get them) and dairy products.

- Men had many responsibilities, but women held considerable authority, too.

How Did the Vikings Fight?

Make no mistake about it, the Viking Age was a violent time. Just consider these two quotes from the *Hávamál*, a collection of sayings supposed to have come from the god Odin himself:

> *"Let the man who opens a door be on the lookout for an enemy behind it."*

> *"A man should never move an inch from his weapons when out in the fields, for he never knows when he will need his spear."*

That second piece of advice was followed even in death: During the pagan era, warriors often were buried with their weapons and armor.

VIKING VOCAB

Breidox: Broad-axe

Bygd: District in Norway, based around military service

Herad: District in Denmark, based around military service

Hird: King's loyal bodyguards

Hoggspjot: Striking spear

Holmganga: Formal duel

Scramasax: Short, single-bladed sword

Skeggox: Beard-axe

Thing: Assembly of freemen

A favorite weapon was the axe, which had actually been out of style in European warfare for decades before the Vikings brought it back with a vengeance. Useful for splitting shields as well as skulls, it concentrated the power of a blow in a relatively small area. One type of axe was known as a *skeggox* or beard-axe because a portion of the blade extended straight downward. Around the year 1000, the *breidox* or broad-axe—with a wider, symmetrical, curving blade—came into use.

The spear, either thrown or handheld, was especially important when warriors were massed together in a "shield wall" such as the "pig nose array"—a blunted-wedge formation believed to have been invented by Odin. Some spears were "winged" with a crossbar to keep them from penetrating the target too deeply and getting stuck. Others were meant to weigh down the defender's struck shield and make it useless; these had intentionally weak shafts that would bend on impact so they couldn't be thrown back. One type that was popular in western Norway was the *hoggspjot*, or striking spear; short-handled and wide-bladed, it could hack as well as stab and was especially useful in ship-to-ship combat.

The sword, however, was considered the pinnacle of weaponry. Celebrated in sagas and legends, swords were given names such as Leggbiti (Leg Biter), Gram (Angry), and Hneitir (Wounder). (Axes might have names, too, but these were usually names of she-trolls and giantesses—Vigglod and Battle-Bright, for example.) The short, single-bladed scramasax sword in use at the beginning of the Viking Age soon gave way to a double-edged broadsword, with a blade around 32 inches long. (The scramasax stuck around a bit longer in Norway.) Made with a "fuller," or groove down the center to reduce weight, this kind of swords was often forged by a method called "pattern welding." Several square rods were twisted individually like sticks of licorice and then hammered together to form a flexible core. Harder iron that could keep an edge was added to the outside. The most prized swords came from the Frankish kingdoms (today's countries of France, Germany, Belgium, and the Netherlands), with the very best blades bearing the maker's mark, "ULFBERHT" or "INGELRII." Norse craftsmen often

Arms and armor of the Vikings

decorated these foreign imports with elaborate bronze hilts inlaid with gold and silver.

Rounding out the Viking armament were single-edged knives and bows and arrows. Equipped with broad, iron-headed arrows, archers were crucial to success in sea warfare or when besieging a walled town. Einar Thambarskelfir (Belly Shaker), a legendary archer and later Jarl of Hladir in Norway, may have gotten his name from the way men's stomachs shook with fear when they saw him drawing his bow.

Shields and helmets offered the best protection. Shields were round and wooden, often colorfully painted. Sometimes edged with leather and reinforced by iron staves in back, they were held with one hand from inside the shield's central "boss," or curve. Helmets were cone shaped, made of iron or leather, and some had nose and eye guards. Well-to-do warriors and nobles were among the few who could afford mail coats made of interlinked iron rings. Early on, this armor came down to the waist, but by the end of the Viking Age it often reached below the knees—and could be exhausting to wear for very long!

NORSE NOTES

Sorry, not a horn to be seen! Artists in the nineteenth century, not the Vikings themselves, were the ones who added horns to Viking helmets, based on Celtic and ceremonial Scandinavian helmets dating back to the Bronze Age.

Battle usually began with a sky-darkening hail of arrows, followed by a flurry of thrown spears as opposing lines of warriors closed in on each other. When armies clashed, it became a bloody scrum of hand-to-hand fighting until one side turned tail and fled.

Even apart from Viking raids, violence and warfare touched everyday Norse life in many ways. Kingdoms were divided into districts that were responsible for contributing a certain number of men and ships for military service when called upon. Called a *herad* in Denmark and a *bygd* in Norway, each district had its own representative assembly of freemen (called a "thing"). A king was nothing without his *hird*, or bodyguards; these men had sworn allegiance to him alone, and they formed the elite core of his army and royal power. A strong and loyal armed retinue was even more important than a blood claim to the throne, and smart kings kept their hird well rewarded with weapons, armor, food, amusements, and treasure.

Violence was also a way of settling legal disputes or points of honor. In traditional duels, the opponents would be sent to a small island or a cordoned-off area to fight it out. Called a *holmganga* or "island going," such a duel involved lots of rules.

Unresolved disputes (and even some that appeared to be resolved) could snowball into bloody feuds between families, lasting for generations.

Were There Women Warriors?

Were there female Vikings? There's a good chance there were a few. Women warriors, such as the proud valkyrja Brynhild (see Otter's Ransom, Sigurd, and the Cursed Treasure, page 109) and the brave shieldmaiden Hervor, who wielded her father's magical sword, *Tyrfing,* feature in many sagas. Some would say we shouldn't trust these stories, since they have supernatural elements like fairy tales do. However, tales that deal more with "real life," like the *Saga of Eirik the Red* and the *Saga of the Greenlanders,* tell of women who fought alongside their men. Also, the semi-historical chronicle, the *Gesta Danorum* by Saxo Grammaticus, claims a troop of 300 shieldmaidens took the field at the Battle of Bravellir in 750. More recently, archaeologists have confirmed by DNA that at least one woman in Birka, Sweden, was buried with her armor and weapons—just like male warriors were.

THINGS TO TAKE AWAY:

- The Vikings' most common weapons were axes and spears, but swords were the most prized.

- Warfare had a major effect on the organization of society during the Viking Age.

- The Vikings *didn't* wear horned helmets!

How Did People Get Around?

Scandinavians had many different means of transportation during the Viking Age. They walked, of course, and some folks had horses to ride. For big cargoes, they used four-wheeled wagons and carriages—and built bridges to support these vehicles over marshy ground and river fords. In wintertime it was safer to travel overland than going by sea, so if there was snow, horse-drawn sledges (carts with runners) and even cross-country skis were put to good use. People even glided across frozen lakes on ice skates made of carved bones strapped to their feet.

NORSE NOTES

Their short, sturdy horses would look to us like large ponies, but this was the standard size in Europe at the time. Larger horses were bred later to carry heavily armored knights.

But it was their legendary ships—and their skill in using them—that allowed the Vikings to make the far-reaching raids and voyages of discovery that have fired the imaginations of generations. Without these ships, the Norsemen might have been just another barbarian group that popped up to trample on the tapestry of European history and then disappeared, like the Huns or the Avars. It was their ships that made the Vikings special.

Viking ships were built hull first, not frame first like other ships at that time. Oak strakes (the horizontal planks that made up the hull) overlapped each other and were fastened together with iron rivets; pitch-soaked wool ropes between the strakes kept out the water. Slender willow branches, strong yet bendy, fastened the interior frame to the hull. The keel was a single heavy oak log running the length of the ship's bottom.

Parts of a Viking longship

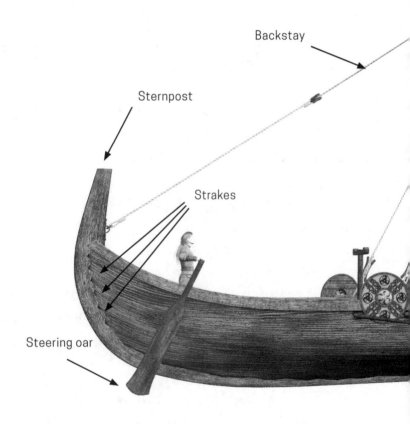

Backstay

Sternpost

Strakes

Steering oar

This arrangement gave a ship great flexibility as well as great strength. The overlapping strakes stopped the ship from plunging too deeply when it dropped down from the swell of large waves, allowing it to glide gracefully and safely over the rough waves of the northern seas. These ships also had very

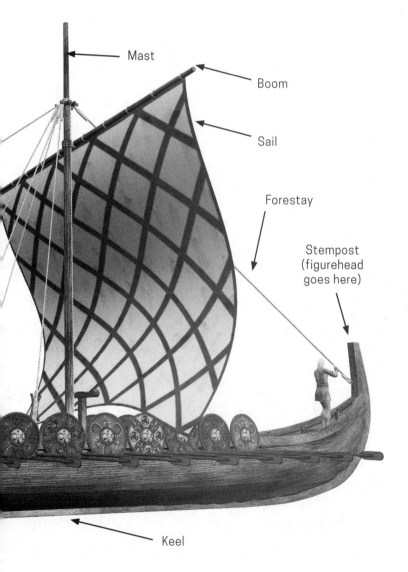

Mast

Boom

Sail

Forestay

Stempost
(figurehead
goes here)

Keel

shallow drafts—they floated nearly on top of the water rather than very deep, like other ships of the time. This is what allowed the Vikings to raid far inland along shallow rivers and estuaries.

VIKING VOCAB

Keel: Heavy oak log at the bottom of a ship's hull

Knorr: Merchant ship around 53 feet long

Snekkja: Warship around 55 feet long

Skeid: Warship over 95 feet long

Strakes: Horizontal planks that make up a ship's hull

The most famous Viking ship was their vessel of war: the longship. From archaeological finds all over Scandinavia, we know that longships varied quite a bit in size. (Some fairly complete specimens can be seen in museums in Oslo, Norway, and in Roskilde, Denmark.) Perhaps the most common type was the *snekkja*, about 55 feet long and only 8 feet wide. Such a ship could hold as many as 30 warriors and rowers, with all their gear. The *skeid* was a much larger war galley/sailing ship, more than 95 feet long and some 14 feet wide; this ship could carry up to 100 men and travel at a speed of over 20 mph! The sagas tell us that around the year 1000, King Olaf Tryggvason of Norway had a ship built that was perhaps 130 feet long. Called the *Long Serpent*, it had benches for 68 rowers and was ornately carved and gilded.

Walrus hides were a crucial resource for shipbuilding. The hide had to be cut away from the animal the way you'd peel an apple: around and around, carefully keeping a single thin spiral. These long strips were braided together to form exceptionally strong cables.

Having strong men at the oars was important when the wind was low—when speeding to attack a town in a sheltered fjord or bay, for instance, or navigating a narrow river. But the Norsemen didn't seem to use their rowing power to ram enemy ships. Combat at sea instead involved crowding all your ships near the king's ship (always the biggest one) and lashing them together to form a floating battlefield. Saga accounts of battles involving a hundred or more ships on each side are probably not terribly exaggerated, though most clashes involved smaller numbers. Fighting between the opposing fleets would proceed pretty much the way it did on land, with arrows flying, infantry charging, and swords flashing.

It was customary for longships to bear fearsome figureheads, such as dragons or bison, supposedly to protect the crew from sea monsters; these were removed when the ships neared shore to avoid angering the spirits of the land.

Built for very different purposes were the Norse merchant vessels. The largest of these was the *knorr*, an ocean-going trader about 53 feet long and 14 feet wide that could hold 24 tons of cargo. It required a crew of only five to eight men and relied almost entirely on sail power for propulsion. (It did have a pair of oars for maneuvering in a harbor.) Smaller vessels—with sails, oars, or both—were used for coastal trading and fishing.

Norsemen were capable sailors, but evidence shows that most voyagers stuck close to shore if they could. It's true that they knew how to read the heavens to maintain their latitude, and how to look for signs of approaching land, but any trip across open water could turn treacherous very quickly. The sagas are overflowing with accounts of mariners lost at sea and ships wrecked on hostile shores or blown far off course by storms. Still, ships were indispensable for connecting the widespread peoples of Scandinavia and their even more far-flung settlements.

The importance of ships during the Viking Age can't be over-stated. They provided transportation for armies, goods, and families. They were praised in song and story and served as status symbols for chieftains and kings. Sometimes royalty and other prominent individuals were actually buried in their ships beneath mounds of earth—as at Tune, Gokstad, and Oseberg in Norway. In other cases, rather than disposing of such a valuable possession, a ship-shaped arrangement of stones decorated a grave. But the image of a ship carrying a dead Viking out to sea—a floating funeral pyre under a rain of fire-arrows—is another fantasy perpetuated by Hollywood. If they'd done that every time a warrior died, the living members of Viking expeditions wouldn't have had any way of getting home!

THINGS TO TAKE AWAY:

- The Norsemen had many ways of getting around, including horses, wagons, sledges, skis, and—most importantly—their marvelous ships.

- Viking ships were strong, flexible, graceful, and fast, with shallow drafts that let them navigate inland waterways.

- Ships were status symbols that a very few important Norsemen even took with them to the grave.

Did the Norse People Write Anything?

Much of what we know about the Viking Age comes from accounts by outsiders (such as Christian missionaries and Arab traders), or it was written down by Scandinavians themselves, but not until much later. But archaeology—especially discoveries in the last 60 years—has revealed that literacy was much more widespread among the Norse people than was previously thought.

Runes

The word "rune" comes from an Old Norse term meaning "secret" or "magical lore." That is surely what these symbols must have seemed like to the northern Germanic people who began using them around the first century AD. We're not sure if rune characters were modeled on the Etruscan, Latin, or Greek alphabet, or all of these, but the runes in use before the Viking Age were organized into an alphabet we call the "Elder Futhark." The word *futhark* comes from the first six characters of the runic alphabet, which was made up of 24 runes—all written with vertical and diagonal strokes. Every rune had its own name and meaning, besides denoting a particular sound. For instance, *Fehu* (cattle) signifies "wealth" and indicates the sound "F." Beyond being a means of communication, in sagas and poems, heroes and gods often used runes to cast magical spells. There is also some evidence that they were used to read fortunes.

NORSE NOTES

Historians have deduced that horizontal lines were avoided for the rune characters because, when carved on wood, they might be mistaken for the grain of the wood.

After 800, during the Viking Age proper, the system evolved into a "Younger Futhark" of 16 runes; around the year 1000, three dotted runes were added, bringing the total to 19. Almost all of these runes only have a single vertical stroke, to make carving them quicker. Because there were fewer runes, some of them had to stand for more than one sound. For example, the Rune "Y" could be used for the "K" sound (or hard "C") and also for a hard "G." There were regional differences, too—and there was no standard spelling! To further complicate matters, writers used abbreviations, and word spacing and punctuation were inconsistent. This all combines to make deciphering runic messages a bit of an art, and experts don't agree on every interpretation.

THE YOUNGER FUTHARK: A RUNE ALPHABET		
RUNE	LETTER	PRONUNCIATION
ᚠ	F	F as in "fun"
ᚢ	U	U as in "tune" or O as in "pole"
ᚦ	TH	TH as in "bath" or "the"
ᚨ	A	A as in "father"
ᚱ	R	R as in "run" (beginning or middle of word)
ᚴ	K	K as in "kick"
ᚼ	H	H as in "hill"
ᚾ	N	N as in "nut"
ᛁ	I	I as in "pin" or EE in "beet"
ᛆ	A	A as in "bag"
ᛋ	S	S as in "sun"
ᛏ	T or D	T as in "tin" or D as in "dog"
ᛒ	B or P	B as in "boy" or P as in "pot"
ᛘ	M	M as in "man"
ᛚ	L	L as in "log"
ᛦ	R	R as in "her" (end of word)
ᛖ	E	E as in "peg"
ᚷ	G	G as in "gum"
ᛂ	Y	OO as in "book"

We know that kings had runes carved on stone to commemorate their relatives and to puff up their accomplishments. Lesser nobles and prominent families did the same thing, often memorializing kin who'd fallen in battle or disappeared on an expedition, so that the runestone became a sort of death certificate or obituary. Some of these stones are very large and incredibly ornate, incorporating runic inscriptions into flowing bands intertwined with scenes from Norse mythology. Runestones are numerous in Sweden and Denmark, but less common in Norway.

VIKING VOCAB

Futhark: Runic alphabet

Runakefli: Rune stick

Rune: Symbol used for writing

Archaeological finds of hundreds of *runakefli* (rune sticks) in Norway, at Bergen and Trondheim, have brought to light just how common writing was. Many of these were tags to indicate ownership of goods ("Eystein owns me"); others were simple messages ("Kiss me") or prayers. Most of these runakefli date from after the Viking Age, but they show that reading and writing weren't reserved for just the wealthy and upper classes. They also tell us that runes were still written and understood by everyday folk in the fifteenth century and even later. Runic inscriptions in wood, bone, metal, or stone—on personal objects, as graffiti on buildings, and so on—have been found almost everywhere the Vikings sailed, from Greenland to Constantinople (modern-day Istanbul in Turkey).

Runestones

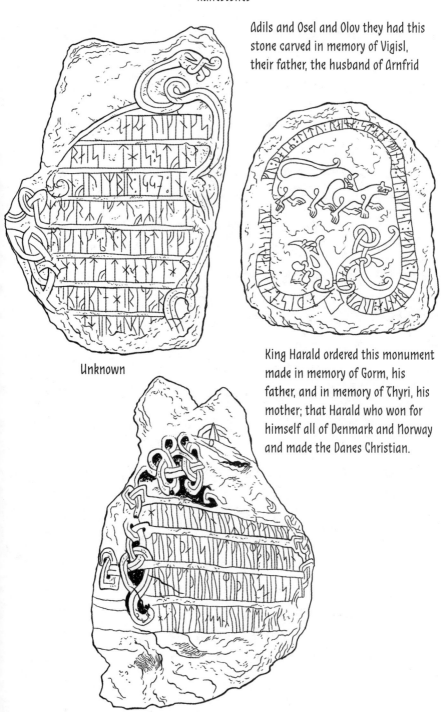

Adils and Osel and Olov they had this stone carved in memory of Vigisl, their father, the husband of Arnfrid

Unknown

King Harald ordered this monument made in memory of Gorm, his father, and in memory of Thyri, his mother; that Harald who won for himself all of Denmark and Norway and made the Danes Christian.

Sagas

Quick: Which European country produced the largest body of prose in its native language during the Middle Ages? Was it France? Italy? England? It may surprise you to learn that it was Iceland. Yes, the farmers and tradesmen of that island out in the North Atlantic are responsible for passing down the overwhelming majority of what we know about the Norse gods, ancient Germanic heroes, and Viking Age kings—along with the workings of their own fascinating society.

Norse settlers first arrived in Iceland sometime in the latter part of the ninth century. Perhaps it was the natural desire of immigrant communities to hold on to their past, or perhaps it was those long winters with little else to do, but between the twelfth and fourteenth centuries the Icelanders preserved—on calfskin and sheepskin—dozens and dozens of "sagas" (literally "that which is said, a story"), and for that we should be thankful. The sagas also preserved most of the Norse poems that we still have, often quoted in the middle of a story for effect.

Written in the Latin alphabet introduced by Christian priests, using the Old Icelandic dialect of Old Norse, these sagas can be broken down into several broad types. There were the Family Sagas, intimately detailing the everyday lives, legal cases, and feuds of the Icelanders—sometimes following families and their drama for generations. There were the King Sagas, chronicling the bloody history of the kings of Norway and their quests for power. There were Sagas of Times Past (*Förnaldarsogur*), fantastic tales of legendary heroes. And there were also Bishops Sagas, Outlaw Sagas, Saints Sagas, and Sturlunga Sagas.

The Sturlunga Sagas, focusing on a particular powerful clan, dealt with the thirteenth-century strife that eventually brought about the end of the Old Icelandic Free State. A major figure in these tales was Snorri Sturluson (1179–1241), an important chieftain and the most famous of the *sagamenn,* or story-tellers. He's responsible for the voluminous work known as *Heimskringla,* a history of the Norwegian kings that reaches into the mythic past and continues through to the Early Middle Ages. Snorri also wrote the *Prose Edda* (see the next section). Snorri's politics, however, didn't endear him to King Haakon IV back in Norway. The king sent men to murder the old chieftain at his home in Reykholt, Iceland, in 1241.

Eddas

The word *edda* comes from the Old Norse word for "great-grand-mother." Eventually it also came to mean "poetics," which is the subject of two extremely important collections of literature, the *Poetic Edda* and the *Prose Edda.* The various manuscripts from which these two works were constructed were written in the thirteenth century, then rediscovered by scholars in the sixteenth and seventeenth centuries. It seems that both of these eddas were meant to preserve lore that was in danger of being lost forever.

First we have the *Poetic Edda*, also called the *Elder Edda*, a collection of poems (and a few bits of prose) that deal with mythology, moral concepts, and stories of northern heroes reaching back to the Migration Period—roughly the years AD 300 to 700. The writers are anonymous, but based on the language used, the poems originated as far back as the ninth century. They were then passed down by word of mouth and brought by Norwegian settlers to Iceland, where they were finally set down on vellum (parchment made from calf skin).

VIKING VOCAB

Edda: Collection of literature dealing with poetry

Kenning: Poetic term used to refer to something else

Skald: Poet

The most famous poem in this collection is "Voluspa" ("The Prophecy of the Seeress"), which tells—often in not very clear terms—about the origins of gods and men, the war between the gods, the death of Odin's son Baldr, and the eventual doom of the gods at Ragnarok. The "Hávamál" ("Sayings of the Highest One")—the longest poem—is a listing of the wisdom of Odin, chief of the gods. In this work, Odin lays down rules for correct and honorable behavior, and also recounts the rune magic he's acquired through his own self-sacrifice. The remainder of the *Poetic Edda* is filled with tales of the gods—particularly Thor's adventures among the giants—and legendary heroes and heroines such as Sigurd the dragon slayer and Brynhild the valkyrja.

The *Prose Edda* is also known as the *Younger* or *Snorri's Edda*, because it was written in about 1220 by our friend Snorri Sturluson, the Icelandic chieftain and master of sagas. It is essentially a textbook for skalds (poets). Writing in prose (as well as using examples from verses by other poets), Snorri explains for future generations the mythological background behind the allusions and terms in traditional Old Norse poetry. It opens with what he called "Gylfaginning" ("The Deluding of Gylfi"), telling the story of the origin and end of the world, as well as a description of their concept of the universe. Snorri softens this for his Christian audience by explaining that the Aesir gods were simply heroes from Troy who'd been elevated to godlike status through years of retelling their stories.

"Skaldskaparmal" ("The Language of Poetry"), another part of the *Prose Edda*, is a conversation between Aegir, god of the sea, and Bragi, god of poetry. Various myths are recounted, but most important is the story of how poetic inspiration came into the world. The section ends with a kind of thesaurus of terms used in poetry. Finally, there's "Hattatal" ("The List of Verse Forms"), the section that's most like a textbook, with hundreds of examples of rhyming schemes, alliteration, meter, and stanza forms—all the rules you'd need to know if you wanted to become a court poet in the Early Middle Ages.

"Kennings" are one of the most distinctive aspects of Old Norse poetry, and you can't begin to understand it without them. A kenning is simply a term used to refer to something else—just as we might say "ship of the desert" to mean "camel." For the Norse people, most of these terms came from tales of gods and heroes. Some are fairly obvious, such as "corpse dew" for "blood" or "steel torrent" for "battle." But others require more in-depth knowledge of myths and legends, such as "Draupnir's precious sweat" to mean "gold," and "Odin's mead" for "poetry." It almost seems as if poets were competing to see who could cram the most obscure references into their verses. The meanings of some kennings have been lost and remain a mystery to us today.

THINGS TO TAKE AWAY:

- Runic writing was widely understood until long after the Viking Age.
- Much of what we know about Norse mythology, as well as ancient stories of kings and heroes, comes from tales that were written down by Icelandic farmers.
- In order to understand Norse poetry, you need to know your mythology.

The History of the Viking Age

Where did the Vikings raid—and how did things change over time?

There was no "one size fits all" for Viking attacks. Depending on whether they were going against the various kingdoms of the British Isles, the waxing and waning Frankish Empire, or the Slavic tribes of Eastern Europe, Vikings had to adapt to the local military and political circumstances to be successful—and very often they weren't. Over three centuries, the character of the raids changed dramatically, sometimes becoming bigger and bigger until they were full-scale invasions by armies led by kings; other times, the Vikings settled down, got married, and simply melted away into the native populations.

The British Isles

When Vikings descended on the British Isles in the late-eighth century, there was no England, Scotland, or Ireland. Instead of the countries we know today, there were seven squabbling Anglo-Saxon kingdoms (Northumbria, Mercia, East Anglia, Kent, Essex, Sussex, and Wessex), five quarreling Irish high kings with numerous rebellious sub-kings, and various regions ruled by the chieftains of the Picts, Welsh, Gaels, and Cornish. Even with flotillas of only a dozen ships or so, Viking raiders—mainly Danes and Norwegians—found the region's isolated coastal towns and monasteries to be easy pickings. They were able to smash, burn, grab, and be gone before any local force could get its act together, and it was almost unheard of for neighboring kingdoms to offer each other any sort of aid. Every now and then a king or army would manage to build barriers or drive off attackers. But for the most part, Vikings could choose their targets without much fear of retaliation.

The tide of these small raids on Britain rose and fell throughout the ninth century, depending on which areas looked the weakest when spring rolled around. That all changed in the year 865. That's when the Great Army of Norse warriors led by three Danish brothers—Halfdan, Ubbi, and Yngvar (Ivar) the Boneless—landed in East Anglia, on Britain's east coast. The difference was that this time it wasn't a raid—it was a conquest.

The Great Army probably numbered well over a thousand warriors. Legend tells us that this "heathen" army was out to avenge the death of the brothers' father, Ragnar, who'd been thrown into a snake pit by King Aella of Northumbria in northern Britain. At the hands of the invaders, King Aella got to experience the Blood Eagle ritual firsthand. The Danes made York their capital (they called it Jorvik back then), and it remained a center of Scandinavian power in England for the next century.

Over the next few years, the Great Army returned to East Anglia, but this time they overran the land and killed the king. According to legend, King Edmund (who later became a saint) was tied to a tree and executed with dozens of Viking arrows. In 874, the Great Army moved on into the Midlands and smashed the Kingdom of Mercia. They took over all the lands to the east and north, from London to the lands south of Northumbria (excluding Wales)—a region that became known as the Danelaw. Wessex, in the extreme southwest of Britain, was the last remaining Anglo-Saxon kingdom—but the Danes were coming for it.

Luckily for Wessex and English history in general, Alfred had ascended to the throne in 871. Following an invasion led by Guthrum, commander of the Great Army in southern Britain,

Alfred fell back. But in 878 he gathered his forces and coun-terattacked at Edington and again at Chippenham. Defeated, Guthrum sued for peace. He agreed to withdraw to the north and to be baptized as a Christian.

That wasn't the end of the menace, of course. For the rest of his life, Alfred (now called "the Great") would have to mount a vigorous defense to keep the Danes at bay and hold on to his kingdom. This included building fortifications and a fleet of large ships. Alfred's son, Edward the Elder, and his daughter, Ethelflaed (the so-called "Lady of the Mercians"), continued this strategy and pushed on into the Danelaw region.

It was an uphill battle, but the West Anglo-Saxons were slowly becoming "English" together, and their land was becoming a single "England." This unity and show of strength made the country an unattractive target for attacks, so the Vikings tended to go elsewhere. Even the Norsemen up in York accepted the rule of the English kings after their own ruler, the Norwegian Eirik Bloodaxe, was deposed and killed in 954.

After a generation grew up without experiencing a Viking raid, an impetuous 12-year-old boy named Aethelred became king of England in 978—and the work of Alfred the Great and his descendants started unraveling. Sensing weakness, Vikings once again plundered the English coasts and countryside. This time, however, the raids had the full royal backing of the cunning Danish king Svein Forkbeard, along with the powerful chieftain Olaf Tryggvason, who would one day rule Norway. The two would later be rivals, but for the 980s and 990s they were united in their aim to bleed as much wealth out of the English as they could. And bleed them the Vikings did. In addition to the treasures they lost through violence, for decades the English were forced to pay enormous amounts in *danegeld* (bribes) to keep the Norsemen away: 16,000 pounds of silver in 994; 24,000 pounds in 1002; 36,000 pounds in 1007; and 48,000 pounds in 1012.

VIKING VOCAB

Danegeld: Bribe meant to keep Vikings from attacking

Danelaw: Area of northern England under Viking control

Jorvik: City of York in northern England

On St. Brice's Day in 1002, King Aethelred ("the Unready") did an especially unwise thing that sealed his fate: He ordered the massacre of all the Danes in the Danelaw. Although he didn't have the power to carry this order out inside the Danelaw itself, there were significant killings in border towns and larger cities. Most importantly, King Svein Forkbeard's own sister, Gunnhild, was said to be among the dead. The Danish king retaliated with a vengeance, carrying out a relentless campaign of terror, pillaging, extortion, and eventually a full-on invasion led by his battle-captains, Thorkell the Tall (who would change sides several times and be paid handsomely for each betrayal) and Olaf Haraldsson (later to become the king and patron saint of Norway). To make a long story short, Svein drove Aethelred out and became king of England himself in 1013, only to die a few weeks later. His son Knut (sometimes spelled "Cnut" or even "Canute") battled a returned Aethelred and then Aethelred's son, Edmund Ironside, before he was able to claim the throne for himself in 1016. Knut made himself the master of an empire that included both England and Denmark, and eventually the Orkney Islands and Norway as well.

But the Viking Age wasn't yet over in England. When Edward the Confessor passed away in 1066 without an heir to the English throne, two men of Norse blood made grabs for the prize. The first, Norway's ruthless and far-traveled King Harald Hardradi (sometimes written as "Hardrada," it means "The Hard Ruler"), launched an invasion with 300 ships. But Harold Godwinson, who'd recently been chosen king by the English nobles, ambushed Harald Hardradi's forces at Stamford Bridge near York. The Norwegian king and most of his men were killed, and only 24 ships were needed to take the survivors home. Days later, Duke William of Normandy (a descendant of a Viking named Hrolf—see page 56) landed his longships at Pevensey and defeated an exhausted Harold Godwinson at the Battle of Hastings. And that's how the duke became King William the Conqueror.

Danes would attempt to wrest control of the island from William for the next 20 years, but the heavy-cavalry-using, French-speaking Normans—no longer Norsemen—had become the firm rulers of England.

WHAT ABOUT IRELAND AND SCOTLAND?

Viking forays into Ireland, Scotland, and the surrounding islands eventually took on a somewhat different character, although at first they seemed similar to the attacks on England. They began with bloody sacks of church properties in

795, and attacks continued for 50 years without any coordinated response from the locals. But then the Vikings—mainly Norwegians—established permanent fortified camps all over Ireland, in such places as Dublin, Waterford, Wexford, and far up the Shannon River at Limerick. Settling down made them more vulnerable to attack, and the Norse enclaves were pulled into Irish politics and even pitted against one another. By 874 their power had waned, and many Vikings took to the seas to find easier game. Thus began what the Irish call the "Forty Years Rest" from Viking raids.

Vikings returned to Ireland in droves after 914, when they found it difficult to ply their "trade" in resurgent England and Francia. They built up the old strongholds that had now become towns. For the better part of a century, their leaders would try, unsuccessfully, to join their Irish possessions with the Kingdom of York in Britain. Tradition holds that King Brian Boru of Munster broke the power of the Dublin Vikings at the Battle of Clontarf in 1014, although he died in the fray. The truth is that constant military pressure and assimilation did the Vikings in. Intermarriage with the locals was common. The Norse settlers converted to Christianity and adopted the Gaelic language. These former Vikings were as likely to be found fighting each other as fighting the Irish, from whom they eventually became indistinguishable.

Scotland saw a similar pattern of Norse settlement mixed with raiding. The Celtic population in the outer islands was overrun by the Vikings, but close proximity with the Celts led the invading Norse people early on to be converted to Christianity. In time, they forged the powerful Jarldom (Earldom) of Orkney, loosely ruled from Norway; under Jarl Sigurd the Stout, it eventually included all of northern Scotland as well as the islands of the Inner and Outer Hebrides. While the Vikings were conducting raids on their near neighbors, the Picts, Britons, and Anglo-Saxons, the Gaelic Scots of Dalriada in western Scotland were left free to overrun the rest of the country—and thus to establish the Kingdom of Scotland in 973.

Western Europe

Danes had been raiding the lands of their neighbors to the south since before their ships had sails. At the dawn of the Viking Age, however, they had to contend with a new power that wouldn't take such behavior lying down: the Frankish Empire under Charlemagne. He built coastal forts and stationed fleets to protect his territories on the North Sea. After Charlemagne's death in 814, his son Louis the Pious at first maintained solid coastal defenses, but these started to crack after 830 as the Franks had to deal with their own internal strife. Four times the Vikings rowed up the Rhine River and sacked the richest port in the empire, Dorestad, in what is now the Netherlands. After Louis died in 840, his three sons— Charles the Bald, Lothar (also spelled Lothair), and Louis the German—split the empire into three squabbling parts. The Vikings pounced.

Charles the Bald's kingdom—roughly the area of modern-day France—was hit the hardest. In 845, Vikings sailed up the Seine River in 120 ships and laid siege to Paris. Charles' solution was the same one that England's King Aethelred would employ 150 years later: pay *danegeld* to make the Vikings go away. While this gave him some breathing room, it only encouraged more raids down the line. Charles even hired one band of Vikings to attack another, but the second band bought off the first. It became clear to the populace that local counts could provide speedier response to foreign invaders than the royal forces could. Charles got lucky when the Great Army attacked England in 865, drawing away the attention of every Viking looking for loot, land, and fame.

Charles' brother Lothar employed a different tactic along the Frisian coast—the modern-day country of the Netherlands. He gave Viking chieftains land to settle, provided they would defend it against other raiders. Although this was a gamble on Lothar's part, it proved to be fairly effective, since these Danes now had some of their own skin in the game.

In 844, a fleet of 100 Viking longships sailed from their settlement at the mouth of the Loire River to try their luck in Spain. Finding resistance too stiff in the Christian regions of the northwest, they struck south into the Muslim land known then as the Emirate of Cordoba. They managed to sack the cities of Cadiz and Seville before being crushed by the Muslim army and barely escaping back to Francia. Viking leaders Hastein and Bjorn Ironsides, also based on the west coast of Francia, tried again in 859 with 62 ships. They bounced down the coast of Spain without much luck, hit the Mediterranean, and just kept going. After striking Narbonne and Arles (on the south coast of modern-day France), they headed on to Italy and sacked Pisa, Fiesole, and Luna—convinced that it was Rome—before returning to loot Pamplona in northern Spain. But it turned out

GREENLAND
Furs
Hides
Walrus Ivory

ICELAND
Falcons
Sulfur
Wool

Sea of Norway

Wool

Soapstone

Iron
Soapstone
Timber
Whetstones

Falcons
Fish
Furs

FINLAND

NORWAY

Birka

Novgorod

Silver

North
Sea

SWEDEN

SCOTLAND

DENMARK

Baltic
Sea

Amber

IRELAND

York

Ribe

Slaves

NOVGOROD-KIEV

Dublin

Hedeby

ENGLAND

Dorestad

Kiev

London

Glass
Jewelry

Honey
Silver
Tin
Wheat
Woolens

Paris

Weapons
Wine

FRANKISH KINGDOMS

Wheat

Salt
Wine

Venice

BULGAR KHANATE

Black Sea

**Atlantic
Ocean**

**KINGDOM
OF LEON**

Rome

KINGDOM OF ITALY

Constantinople

UMAYYAD EMIRATE

Brocade
Jewelry
Spices
Wine

Mediterranean Sea

FATIMID CALIPHATE

Cairo

Viking raiding and trading

to be a rough cruise: They limped back to the Loire region in 862 with only 20 ships left.

Alfred the Great's victories against the Danes in Britain in 878 turned out to be bad news for the Franks, as Vikings returned to their shores in search of softer targets. They ravaged up and down the coast of Flanders and the Rhineland for years before pushing up the Seine to Paris once again in 885. With the help of the city's fortified bridges, Bishop Joscelin and Count Odo led a resistance that held out for a year. But when Emperor Charles the Fat came to "relieve" them, he simply allowed the Vikings to sail farther up the Seine. For this, Charles was toppled from his throne and the Frankish Empire was split in two. Odo was chosen as king in the west, and Charles' nephew Arnulf ruled in the east. Their military resolve (and a famine) convinced the Vikings to go elsewhere for a time.

In 911 a Danish Viking named Hrolf made an unsuccessful attack on Chartres, southwest of Paris. Under a peace treaty negotiated with King Charles the Simple, Hrolf converted to Christianity and was made Count of Rouen. As such he was charged with protecting the lower reaches of the Seine from further Viking incursions. He and his descendants accomplished this but also invited more settlers from Scandinavia to join them. They expanded westward toward Brittany, another area of Viking activity. By the early-eleventh century, Hrolf's descendants had taken the title "duke" and their "Northman's Land" had become Normandy. It was known as a place where Scandinavian Vikings could find aid and comfort during their "off-season." Still, like the Norse people in Ireland, they became assimilated into the surrounding culture, taking on its language and religion. When William the Conqueror launched his invasion of England in 1066, the Normans were thoroughly Frenchmen despite their Scandinavian ancestry.

Hrolf was known as "Rollo" to the Franks. His full name was Gongu-Hrolf, or "Hrolf the Walker," because he was too big to ride the horses of that era.

■ ■

Eastern Europe & Beyond

Just as the Danes and Norwegians formed the major part of Viking expeditions to the west, the Swedes took the lead in raiding and trading in Eastern Europe. They were known there as the "Rus," probably from the Old Norse *rodr*, meaning a crew of oarsmen.

VIKING VOCAB

Rus: Scandinavian ruling class in Novgorod and Kiev

Varangian Guard: Scandinavian bodyguards of the Byzantine emperor

Varangians: Norse mercenaries serving the Byzantine emperor

■ ■

The Swedes' activities in this region actually started at least a century before the westerly Viking raids, and by the middle of the eighth century they had a permanent merchant presence on the Baltic coast and around Lakes Ladoga and Onega, in what is now northwest Russia. Besides trading furs and slaves, the Rus had two other motivations for pushing deeper into the region: fine Arabic silver and an extensive network of navigable rivers for their shallow-drafted ships.

By 860 the Rus had established Novgorod (on the Volkhov River, near Lake Ilmen) as their capital, and they set about controlling the routes along the major river systems, including the Dnieper, the Volga, and the Don. Portages—places where ships could be lifted out of the water to be transported a short distance overland to another river—were crucial for connecting the Baltic Sea with both the Black Sea and the Caspian Sea. There, the Rus could trade directly with the Arabs of the Abbasid Caliphate, the Khazar Khanate in the Caucasus, and the Byzantine Empire at Constantinople (after trying a couple of times to conquer that ancient city). Around the year 882, they seized the Slavic town of Kiev on the Dnieper River and made it their capital, ruling a vast territory that would someday become the heart of the Russian state.

The Rus became a military and merchant ruling class over their Slavic subjects, but they were always a very small percentage of the population. Slowly but surely, they lost whatever Scandinavian culture they'd brought with them as they intermarried and accepted Eastern Orthodox Christianity. After the middle of the tenth century, the princes of Kiev all had Slavic names.

A second wave of Norsemen, however, found their cousins the Rus to be hospitable when they moved through the region in the late-tenth century to find employment as mercenaries. Called "Vaeringjar" (men of the pledge), many of these fighting men took service under the Byzantine emperor, forming an elite unit known as the Varangian Guard. An ambitious exiled Norwegian prince named Harald Sigurdsson quickly rose through the ranks to command the Varangians, fighting Arabic pirates in the eastern Mediterranean, conquering the towns of Saracens and Lombards in Sicily and Italy, and even leading an expedition to repair the Church of the Holy Sepulcher in Jerusalem. Covered in glory and riches, Harold took part in a palace coup against the emperor before escaping Constantinople and eventually returning to Norway to become King Harald Hardradi—the "Thunderbolt of the North"—in 1047 (page 51).

THINGS TO TAKE AWAY:

- The Vikings were cunning and opportunistic, taking political instability into account when planning where to attack.

- The Vikings' great advantage was their mobility; when they settled down, they were as vulnerable to attack as everyone else.

- Eventually all the Vikings' overseas settlers were assimilated into the native populations.

- Vikings could find friendly folks who spoke their language in communities all the way from Ireland to the Black Sea.

What Was Happening Back at Home?

The Viking Age was a time of political consolidation in Scandinavia, when smaller territories were joining together into larger kingdoms. Why? The answer is simple: wealth. Treasure was flooding into the Norse homelands from the east, west, and south. Some of this was plunder from raiding, but successful Vikings were also returning home with scores of loyal followers—good to have if you plan on grabbing a throne. The region was a major hub for trade routes that stretched a third of the way around the globe. Controlling trade and collecting taxes might not be as exciting as sacking a town, but it was safer and more reliable. With wealth comes power, and from region to region there were bold Norsemen who understood how to work local circumstances to take control. Some failed initially, while others succeeded only to have power slip away from their descendants, but the trend was unmistakably toward stronger, centralized kingships. The map of Scandinavia was becoming closer to one we would recognize today.

Denmark

Denmark was already an established kingdom at the beginning of the Viking Age, encompassing the Jutland Peninsula, the islands of Fyn and Sjaelland, the southern part of what is now Sweden, and sometimes the Vestfold region of what is now Norway. Godfred, the first Danish king we know anything about, came to power around the year 800. A contemporary of Charlemagne, he vied with the Frankish emperor for control of the trade passing between the Baltic and North seas, as well as up and down the Jutland Peninsula. To this end, he made a show of force with his fleet at the Frisian border and destroyed Reric to the east, a major trading port for Charlemagne's Slavic allies. Furthermore, Godfred improved and expanded defenses throughout the Jutland Peninsula and bolstered fortifications around major market towns. He was determined that all trade goods would pass through Danish hands, or not at all.

Godfred died around 810, setting off a bloody, decades-long conflict among his sons and nephews. At times Denmark had two or more competing kings. The Franks tried to capitalize on this chaos, until they got caught up in their own dynastic troubles after 840. The Danes paid them back in 845 by sending a huge fleet to Hamburg and burning the city. During this time, St. Anskar attempted to bring Christianity north from Saxony, building a church at Hedeby and one up in Birka among the Svear.

We have little concrete knowledge of Denmark's history from 850 to 936. When Unni, the Archbishop of Hamburg-Bremen, visited Denmark in 936 he found an unapologetically pagan king named Gorm the Old firmly in power. Gorm's runestone memorial to his wife Thyri at Jelling in central Jutland featured the first native use of the term "Denmark" that we know about.

Gorm's son, the colorfully named Harald Bluetooth, had a long and ambitious reign marked by adventures abroad and consolidation of power at home. He gained a degree of control over Norway by supporting his sister Gunnhild and her sons in a campaign to retake the Norwegian throne from Hakon the Good around 960. Harald would later turn against them and split Norway with the jarl of the Trøndelag region up north. But an expedition against the Svear in Sweden ended in defeat for Harald at Uppsala in the 980s.

Like his predecessors, Harald had troubles with the German emperors. Otto II crossed the Danevirke, a fortified earthen wall at the base of the Jutland peninsula in 974 and occupied Hedeby. Following a marriage alliance between his son, Svein Forkbeard, and a princess of the Slavic Wends on the Germans' eastern flank, however, Harald sent Svein south to reclaim these lands. To bolster Danish defenses and his own power, in about 980 Harald built a series of symmetrical ring forts throughout the country. He was also the first Scandinavian king to openly embrace and promote Christianity within his realm. He placed his own runestone at Jelling, featuring carved depictions of Christ and a dragon-like beast, as well as an inscription spelling out his own accomplishments.

VIKING VOCAB

Danevirke: A large bank of earth and timber built to defend Denmark's southern border

A few years later in 987, Svein deposed his father and sent him into exile. As we've already seen, he executed a long campaign of harassment and ultimately conquest in England, extracting a great deal of silver in the process (page 49). Svein's son, Knut the Great, ruled an empire that included Denmark, Norway, England, and Orkney in Scotland. Knut was the first

Scandinavian king to be accepted as an equal by the other Christian monarchs of Europe, and he even attended the coronation of Emperor Conrad in Rome in 1027. But things began to fall apart following his death in 1035. Dynastic squabbles ensued and territories were lost and gained, but mostly lost.

The winner of these fights—more by attrition than skill—was Svein Estridsson, the son of Knut's sister. After the 1047 death of Magnus the Good—who'd been king of both Norway and Denmark—Svein was named sole king of Denmark. Norway went to Magnus' uncle, Harald Hardradi, who would be Svein's bitter rival for the rest of his life. Following the Norman Conquest of England (and the death of Harald Hardradi), Svein twice tried to invade that island nation himself, without success. Svein fathered five kings of Denmark and greatly increased state cooperation with the Church. He's sometimes called the last Viking king of Denmark, and sometimes the first medieval king.

Norway

The early story of the rise of royal power in Norway is veiled in a swirl of legends, but even so we can see patterns that remained true throughout the Viking Age. It all started with the kings of the Yngling Dynasty, so called because they claimed descent from Yngvi-Frey—another name for the fertility god Frey. Striving not only for dominance in their fertile home region around Oslofjord in the south, the Yngling kings also sought control of the "North Way" trade route up to Hålogaland. Opposing them were the jarls of Hladir in the Trøndelag region.

And always there were the Danes striving to assert their power from the south.

VIKING VOCAB

Yngling Dynasty: Kings said to be descended from the god Frey

■ ■

A king in the south named Harald Finehair took advantage of Danish weakness near the end of the ninth century to firm up his position and reach for more. After fighting to unite the entire Oslofjord, he made an alliance with Jarl Hakon up in Trondheim by marrying the jarl's daughter. He then went after western Norway, defeating a coalition of kinglets, jarls, and chieftains at the massive sea battle of Hafrsfjord near Stavanger, sometime between 885 and 900 (during the latter half of Alfred the Great's reign in England).

Harald set tolls on trade and established quotas of men, arms, and ships that regional jarls and chieftains had to provide for the realm's defense. He also confirmed the authority of three regional freemen's assemblies to publicly vote royal proclamations up or down. He understood the stability brought by these assemblies: "With law shall the kingdom be built up."

Harald lived into his eighties, reigning for more than 50 years, and he may have fathered as many as 20 sons. The most energetic (if his name is any indication) was Eirik Bloodaxe, who was married to Gunnhild, daughter of Gorm the Old of Denmark. Eirik seized power immediately after Harald's death, but he was quickly challenged by his much younger brother, Hakon the Good, who'd been fostered at the court of King Athelstan in England. Eirik was deposed, fled to York to be king there, came back, and was kicked out again. He finally died in battle—like a good Viking—in 954 at Stainmore, England.

A proclaimed Christian when he left England to return to Norway, Hakon soon found proselytizing to be unpopular in his homeland, so he went back to the old gods. He strengthened the national character of the regional assemblies' laws, making them apply over wider areas. He was able to do these things with the support of the Jarl of Hladir, who got to remain semi-independent.

But Eirik Bloodaxe's sons wanted revenge for their father and a kingdom of their own. Appealing to their other uncle, Harald Bluetooth of Denmark, they got support in the form of an invasion force for attacking the Oslofjord region. Hakon pushed his nephews back and counterattacked in Denmark at Jutland and Sjaelland. The Norse warlords fought a seesaw war for years until Hakon was mortally wounded in a sea battle around 960. He was laid to rest with pagan pomp and circumstance, wearing full armor, in a large burial mound. The leader of Eirik's sons, Harald Greycloak, wasn't able to conquer the entire country nor remain king for very long. Between the Jarl of Hladir to the north and the Danes to the south, he was squeezed into a small region of southwest Norway, where he was just another jarl. Once again Norway was divided and without a king.

A dashing young nobleman named Olaf Tryggvason, great-grandson of Harald Finehair, set out to change that. A true

Viking with a career that included savage raids in the Baltic and taking part in Svein Forkbeard's harrying of England, Harald set out in 995 to become king of all Norway. Rich from all that *danegeld* bribe money and with a fleet manned by veterans, he drove out the Jarl of Hladir and was soon proclaimed king throughout Norway. A recent convert to Christianity, he imported English priests and tried to spread his new faith up and down the coast—and he wasn't too gentle about it. After five years, his enemies gathered a fleet to ambush him at sea. Outnumbered and with his flagship, the *Long Serpent*, about to be boarded, Olaf dove into the frigid waters of the Baltic Sea somewhere between Wendland and Denmark. (As with Elvis, unconfirmed reports of Olaf sightings popped up for years afterward.)

In 1015 another Olaf (Haraldsson, aka "the Stout") would reverse Norway's disintegration. Also a wealthy veteran of Svein's campaigns in England and also a Christian, this stocky Viking quickly conquered land from south to north and installed loyal nobles in positions of power. He also respected the freemen's assemblies and enforced the rule of law. Mostly, however, he is known for vigorously pursuing a policy of conversion to Christianity; he tore down the temples to the pagan gods and set up a state church organization.

But it was a Christian king who eventually moved against him, with some help from Norwegian pagans. Knut the Great of Denmark and England invaded around 1028 and, relatively unopposed, drove out Olaf. Although Olaf returned in 1030, he and his cause died on the field of Stiklarstadir. For his efforts for the faith, however, Olaf was eventually made the patron saint of Norway.

After the death of Knut in 1035, Olaf's young son Magnus returned from refuge in the court of Jaroslav the Wise in Kiev. Quickly proclaimed king in Norway, he headed south and accomplished the same thing in Denmark. But when he died without an heir, power transferred to his ambitious uncle Harald Sigurdsson (aka Hardradi, "The Hard Ruler"). Harald's long reign helped cement the idea of "one king, one Norway." He spent much of his later life trying to conquer Denmark, burning Hedeby to the ground in the process. When Denmark proved unattainable, he struck at England. It was there that he died in battle in 1066—a fitting place to end the Viking Age.

Sweden

We know less about the kings of the Svear and the Gotar at home in Sweden during this time than we do about rulers elsewhere in Scandinavia. The Svear and the Gotar are said to have fought savagely against each other during the legendary times of late prehistory. It appears that the land of the Svear, with its ancient seat of power at Uppsala, was the more dominant—but that didn't translate into the ability to unite the two realms until much later. But the Svear did collect tribute from the Finns, maintained an influence over the trade on the far eastern shores of the Baltic and Russian rivers, and controlled the large islands of Oland and Gotland. It is also reported that around 900 they "seized royal power in Denmark by force of arms."

A King Eirik in the late-tenth century defended his realm against a takeover attempt led by his nephew, Styrbjorn Starki—husband of Thyri, Harald Bluetooth's daughter. With Danish aid, Styrbjorn Starki got as far as Uppsala, but there the Svear forces crushed the invaders, earning Eirik the nickname "Sigrsaell"—the Victorious.

Eirik's son Olaf Skotkonung was the next to appear, in 995. His nickname means "Tributary King," and he may have been under the thumb of Denmark's Svein Forkbeard. Olaf was the first king we know of who ruled over both the Svear and the Gotar, though true unification wouldn't come about until the twelfth century.

King Olaf also converted to Christianity, though few of his subjects did so. Well into the twelfth century, in fact, king and commoner alike—Christian or not—were expected to take part in rituals at the great pagan temple in Uppsala. Offerings of food and drink were made next to huge wooden statues of the gods, and songs of devotion were sung. Every nine years, in a nearby grove, it was customary to sacrifice nine males of eight different kinds of animals—including humans—to nurture the sacred trees. The eleventh-century German missionary Adam of Bremen passed down the testimony of a witness who said he saw men's corpses hanging alongside those of dogs and horses.

Dissatisfaction with their king's new religion was one reason King Olaf was forced to share power with his son, Anund Jakob, and then cede it completely. Father and son (and their descendants) would embroil themselves in alliances and double-crosses with the various kings and jarls of Norway and Denmark, jockeying for supremacy throughout the remainder of the Viking Age.

THINGS TO TAKE AWAY:

- The trend throughout Scandinavia as the Viking Age progressed was for stronger, more centralized kingships.

- Successful kings needed to control not just land, but also trade.

- Marriage and family ties could be incredibly important politically, but were no guarantees of friendly relations between kings.

- By the end of the Viking Age, Christianity had been accepted all over Scandinavia except for parts of Sweden.

What Other Lands Did They Colonize?

The wanderlust that drove the Scandinavians to raid and trade in foreign lands also led them to settle in far-flung places. These tended to be uninhabited or sparsely populated islands across the North Sea and the North Atlantic. Although relations with the locals—and each other—were often far from peaceful, these settlers' reasons for leaving home were the same as those of immigrants across the ages. They were looking for freedom and a plot of land to call their own.

Iceland and the Faeroe Islands

Originally settled by Irish hermits seeking spiritual refuge from the secular world, the Faeroes and Iceland were intruded upon by Norse immigrants around 825 and 870, respectively. Most of these newcomers were from western Norway (the districts of Sogn, Rogaland, and Agder); many had an independent bent and were unhappy with the growth of royal power in their native land. They found good grazing for their flocks on both Iceland and the Faeroes, but not much in the way of suitable land for crops or forests. Actually, the environments were quite similar to what they were used to back in their homeland.

While the Faeroes had come under the direct control of the Norwegian crown by 895, the Iceland colonists set up their own peculiar form of government that lasted quite a bit longer. Chieftain-priests known as *godar* handled local disputes and represented their supporters (*thingmenn*) in the regional assemblies (*things*) and the yearly national assembly, the *Althing*. Only the godar could vote for new laws or appoint judges at the Althing, but they had to take the wishes of their thingmenn into account.

Being a godar wasn't a matter of lineage or class; it was an office that could be bought, sold, traded, and shared, making it a position that almost anyone with ambition and a working knowledge of the rather complex legal system could aspire to. There was no executive branch to enforce the laws—no kings or sheriffs or the like. Private individuals, most often godar and their supporters, ensured that fines were paid to the damaged parties or that sentences for outlawry (banishment and forfeiture of property) were carried out. Naturally, they took a cut of the money that was collected.

This form of government served the Icelanders well, even resolving the contentious debate over the conversion to Christianity via a peaceful compromise around the year 1000. In the thirteenth century, however, political power became concentrated in a few wealthy families, and widespread violence broke out as they vied for control. Some Icelanders appealed to the Norwegian king to step in. He did, and Iceland lost its independence in 1263.

VIKING VOCAB

Althing: Yearly national assembly of Iceland

Godar: Chieftain-priests

Outlawry: Punishment by banishment and forfeiture of property

Thingmenn: Pledged supporters of godar

Greenland

Norsemen first sighted the frigid coast of this vast arctic island around 900, but it took a land shortage in Iceland to persuade Eirik the Red to relocate there. He named the island Greenland in the hope that folks would follow him to build a new society there. They did, and at one time there were some 4,000 Norse people on more than 300 farms spread over three settlements. They raised livestock, hunted for valuable walrus ivory and polar bear furs, and even traded with the native Inuit people. Norway took nominal control of Greenland in 1261.

The climate grew colder after 1300, during what has been called the "Little Ice Age," and relations with the native Inuit people grew strained and often violent as the island's resources dwindled. Without wood to repair or build ships, and with sea ice cutting the Norse settlers off from their home-land for years at a time, they grew more isolated. Ultimately they couldn't adapt to these harsher conditions, and the Norse settlements died out completely by the middle of the sixteenth century.

The New World: Helluland, Markland, and Vinland

In 985 a Norwegian named Bjarni Herjolfsson got lost on his way to Greenland and sighted a mysterious land to the west. When he finally found his way to Eirik the Red's colony on Greenland, he was ridiculed for being too cowardly to explore the new land he'd seen. Fifteen years later, Eirik's son Leif bought Bjarni's ship and set out to do just that. Sailing up the west coast of Greenland, he then headed west and found a flat, glacial land he called Helluland or "Slab Land"—almost certainly Baffin Island at the top of the North American continent. Steering south, he discovered a thickly forested coast that he named Markland—"Wood Land," probably Labrador in what is now Canada. Continuing south, he encountered salmon-rich rivers and woodland brimming with wild grapes; he called this place Vinland, meaning "Wine Land." Possibly he had reached Newfoundland, Nova Scotia, or someplace north of Cape Cod. The explorer stayed a winter there.

VIKING VOCAB

Skraelingar: "Wretches," uncomplimentary term for Native Americans

Leif's voyage was followed by another led by his brother Thorvald, who was killed by a *skraeling* arrow. (*Skraelingar* was an uncomplimentary term for the Native Americans, meaning "wretches.") A Norseman named Thorfinn Karlsefni organized a much larger expedition with the aim of colonizing this new land, but his effort failed after three years of continuous hostility from the natives. Leif's sister Freydis led yet another group to Vinland but had to turn back after a bloody encounter with the natives.

NORSE NOTES

A base used by one of these crews, including a boat repair shed and a blacksmith shop, has been excavated at L'Anse aux Meadows on Newfoundland.

By 1020, the Norse had given up trying to settle North America. But their attempts were recorded in sagas, historical chronicles, and obscure maps, to be discovered by later generations of explorers.

THINGS TO TAKE AWAY:

- The Norse took their own customs and traditional ways of making a living to the new lands where they settled.

- Efforts to colonize Greenland eventually fizzled, and attempts to settle North America failed outright.

A MISCELLANY OF NORSE MYTHS

There are times when Norse mythology seems just like the popular image of the Viking Age itself: rough and violent. From the creation of the world to its fiery end, there is murder, dismemberment, torture, and never-ending warfare. Add in greed, lust, jealousy, revenge, and the occasional incidence of cannibalism, and you have some R-rated stuff.

But that's only part of the picture. Our two most important ancient written sources, the *Poetic Edda* and Snorri Sturluson's *Prose Edda* (see page 43), include stories of incredible courage, steadfast devotion, fervent love, and sly trickery. There are gods willing to sacrifice everything to gain the objects of their desire, heroes bound by honor to finish impossible deeds, and clever dwarfs and giants unmatched in cunning—except possibly by the unpredictable trickster god Loki. For every tragedy, there is comedy; for every tale of drama and despair, there's one of hope and inspiration.

You may find some of the stories strange. Very strange. Not only do the people in these tales have seemingly unpronounceable names, but why they do the things they do can seem downright weird to our modern-day way of thinking. And matters such as time, space, and the supernatural don't always make sense, or they're twisted to suit the tale. To make things even more confusing, two or more characters may share the same name, or—even more common—one character may be called by several names. (We're looking at you, Odin!) It's important to remember that these myths were originally folktales meant to explain why and how the world worked. Most of them were handed down by word of mouth for generations before someone finally wrote them down. Strangeness was bound to creep in somewhere.

The following stories are meant to brush away some of the cobwebs of the last thousand years or so. After you've read these tales and the encyclopedia that follows them, you'll be an expert on the people, places, and things that populate the fantastic world of the Vikings!

The Origin of the Cosmos and the Coming of the Gods

It was at the beginning of time, when nothing was;

Sand was not, nor sea, nor cool waves.

Earth did not exist, nor heaven on high.

The mighty gap was, but no grass.

Before the world came into being, there was only a gap— Ginnungagap, a void of pure nothingness. It was a blank slate, neither light nor dark, good nor evil. Then a spark ignited to the south. That spark became a flame, the flame became a fire, and the fire became an inferno—a boiling, molten world known as Muspelheim. Too hot to touch, too bright even to look at, Muspelheim was the only thing that existed. Then, far to the north, cold and darkness came together where the light and heat of Muspelheim couldn't penetrate. This was Niflheim, the world of darkness. In the middle of Niflheim grew a burbling pool of venom called Hvergelmir, and from this pool flowed many rivers, swift and wide. The farther they flowed from the source, the more ice built up—first in chunks, then becoming icebergs, and finally freezing together at the edge of the gap.

Poisonous vapors came off the ice and froze, too. Over countless eons this toxic frost built up until it had bridged the space between dark Niflheim and bright Muspelheim. Intense cold met intense heat, and there in the middle was a place mild enough to support life. Drops of melting frost took the shape of an enormous man: Ymir, the first frost-giant. He was filthy and evil, as you might expect of someone created from poison, ice, and flame. From the sweat of his armpits came a pair of male and female giants, and his legs mated and gave birth to a son. These three giants shared Ymir's ugly disposition, and they set about making more of their kind.

As time wore on, Ymir's stomach began to rumble with hunger. But just as he was eyeing his children with a hungry look, a cow named Audhumla walked out of the steaming mists. She fed him with four rivers of milk that gushed from her udders. As he drank, she received nourishment by licking salty stones of ice on the edge of the gap. On the first day, her tongue uncovered a patch of hair; the next day, her licking revealed that the hair was attached to the head of a man; and on the third day, his entire body was exposed. The man's name was Buri—the first god. He was big, strong, and handsome, and he wasted no time in getting a wife, who gave him a son named Bor.

When Bor married Bestla, the daughter of the giant Bolthorn, the other giants began to resent sharing their space and their women with these newcomers. Bor and Bestla had sons named Odin, Vili, and Ve. By the time they had all grown to manhood, the jealousy and suspicion between the two groups—the gods and the giants—was turning into outright hatred. Odin saw the looming threat, especially from foul, bloated Ymir, and convinced his brothers to creep up on Ymir and slit his throat. Blood poured from his body in a flood, drowning all of the frost-giants except Bergelmir and his wife, who rode out the flood in a wooden box.

The three gods dragged Ymir's body to the middle of the mighty gap and put it to good use. From his flesh they made the earth, encircled by his blood—the wide sea, the lakes, and the rivers. His bones and teeth became rocks and boulders that they scattered all over this new world. As they were deciding how to cap their creation, they noticed maggots wiggling in the dead giant's flesh. They decided to give them consciousness and the shape of men, and they called them dwarfs. However, they thought it best that these beings continue to live underground, some in dirt and some in rocks. The gods chose four of the dwarfs—Nordri, Sudri, Austri, and Vestri—to hold up Ymir's vast skull, which became the sky. They threw pieces of the giant's brain upward to be clouds.

Their new world needed light, so the gods took sparks from fiery Muspelheim and placed them in the heavens. These were the stars, the sun, and the moon—but they didn't know their places and tended to wander. This upset Odin and his brothers, and as they walked along a beach pondering how to fix this chaos, they came upon a pair of logs. On a whim, they shaped these into people: a man and a woman. Hoping to create a race that would worship and serve the gods, Odin breathed souls and life into the logs. Vili gave them consciousness and movement, and Ve bestowed faces, speech, and senses. The gods clothed them and called them Ask and Embla—the first human beings. They were happy with their new creations but saw that the humans were threatened by the frost-giants, which by now had replenished their numbers. They took the last bit of Ymir's corpse, his eyelashes, and set it up as a protective barrier around the middle of the world, where the humans would live. They called this wall and the land it surrounded Midgard, and the giants were banished to the lands beyond.

The gods then turned back to the problem of the lights in the sky. They found Nott, the daughter of a giant, who was as dark as Niflheim. They had her and her son, Dag, drive their chariots across the sky to split each day into cycles of light and darkness.

The sun and the moon were also in the sky, but they wandered to and fro in an unruly way. The problem resolved itself when the gods discovered that a man named Mundilfaeri had named his daughter and son Sol and Mani, after the sun and moon. The gods punished him by taking away his children and having them drive the actual sun and moon through the sky in their chariots every day and every night. Now the world had a way to measure the passage of time. Unfortunately, a pair of monstrously hungry wolves named Skoll and Hati, born to a giantess in the far-off forest of Ironwood, decided to pursue the sun and moon until the end of time.

As both humans and giants multiplied, so did the gods. Odin had a son with Jord, the daughter of Nott; his name was Thor. Other gods included Hoenir, Mimir, Tyr, and Heimdall. They were also joined by Loki, whose father was the giant Farbauti. The other gods didn't trust this handsome newcomer with the mischievous smile, but Odin convinced them to let him stay. Odin married Frigg, the daughter of Fjorgvin, and they ruled as king and queen of the Aesir—the whole assembly of gods and goddesses.

Odin and Frigg fortified a place in the heavens known as Asgard. In the middle of Asgard was the plain of Idavoll, where they built magnificent halls and temples out of precious metals. This was also where the tree known as Yggdrasil, or the world-ash, had sprouted. Yggdrasil's roots connected the nine worlds, from Niflheim to the highest heaven—a fragile framework on which the entire order of the cosmos depended.

This began a Golden Age. The gods were happy and had everything they desired. They laughed and played games with gold pieces as they lay on the green grass. The world was at peace.

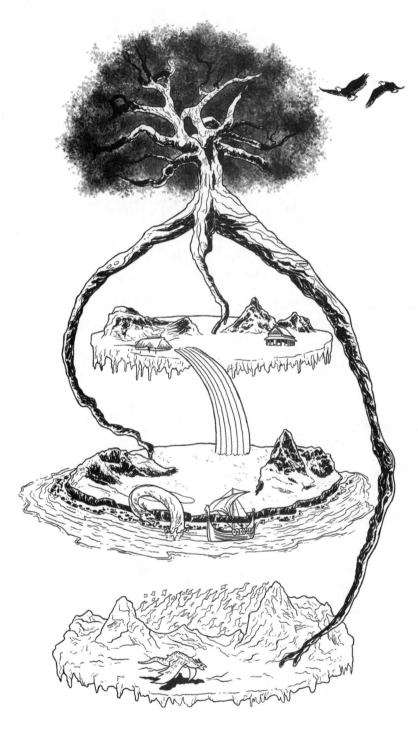

Yggdrasil, the World-Ash Tree, and the Norse universe

Then one day three sisters appeared at the well near the world-ash. They had come from Jotunheim, the world of the giants. The Aesir could sense the immense power of these goddesses—called "norns"—and they were afraid. They knew that Fate had now come into the world, and not even the gods could escape it.

Loki and the Builder

The world's first war was between the Aesir and another group of gods, called the Vanir. No one is sure what started it, whether it was the Aesir's violent treatment of a witch named Gullveig, or perhaps jealousy over how many human worshippers each group had. The war ended when the two armies exchanged hostages and swore pledges of truce. Peace reigned once more.

However, the fighting had reduced the walls of Asgard to rubble. Asgard was vulnerable to attacks by giants, especially since Thor was away in the east, bashing trolls (he was trying out his new hammer, but more about that later). As luck would have it, a builder showed up and claimed he could do the job in a mere three seasons. The gods were naturally suspicious about who this builder was, especially when he told them his price for the work: the sun, the moon, and the hand of Freyja—goddess of love—in marriage.

The gods knew they couldn't afford this, no matter how badly they needed their defenses intact. But Loki urged them to reconsider. "Look, all we need to do is place some heavy restrictions on him—how long he has, what kind of help he can get, and so on—and if he doesn't finish on time, we pay him nothing."

"And what if he does finish on time?" asked Freyja.

"He won't," Loki assured her. "I would stake my life on it."

The gods told the builder that they'd pay him what he asked, but only if he completed the walls in one winter and did it with no one helping him. The builder considered this at length before asking, "Could I use my horse, Svadilfaeri, to help me haul the stone?"

"Let him," whispered Loki to Odin. "It won't make one bit of difference."

And so the gods allowed the builder his horse, and they all swore oaths to seal the deal. On the first day of winter, a rumbling awoke the gods. Peering out from his silver hall called Valaskjalf, Odin saw the cause: The builder was leading his enormous horse, which was dragging a sledge weighed down with a mountain of granite. The ground shook as the builder tipped over his load of stone. He set about shaping the blocks and putting them in place at a speed that amazed even the gods.

So it went, day after day, and the walls grew ever higher. The pace worried Odin. He and Tyr went out to inspect the fortifications, hoping to find flaws, but they both agreed that the walls were indeed tall enough and strong enough to resist an assault by giants, gods, or any other being living in the nine worlds. With three days to go before the first day of summer, it looked as though the builder would easily complete his task on time. The gods held an emergency assembly in their golden hall of Gladsheim to decide what could be done. Freyja, understandably, was especially furious.

"This is all your fault, Loki!" she yelled at him. "If I have to marry this man, you won't live to see the wedding! Remember what you staked."

"I believe I said I *would* stake my life on it, not that I actually *was* staking my life," he replied smugly. "And you should remember that we have many laws against killing our own—"

"*Within* the walls of Asgard," Odin interrupted, "but for the time being, anyway, we don't have completed walls. Or we could take you outside to do the deed. Or I could devise a hideous punishment to torment your immortal body until the end of time. What I'm saying is that our options are many, but yours are not."

Loki knew Odin was serious, and he'd better find a solution, fast. He went out to watch the builder work, hoping an idea would come to him. Perhaps if he killed the man, or at least maimed him so he couldn't work? No—more of those blasted sworn oaths and laws. Then he noticed: Svadilfaeri wasn't just a horse, he was a stallion. Loki's mind went where only Loki's mind could go.

The next dawn, as the builder and Svadilfaeri were hauling what looked to be the last load of stone needed to finish the wall, a beautiful mare galloped out of the nearby forest and crossed their path. Svadilfaeri saw her, caught a whiff of her, and went mad. He bucked and jumped, tearing his lead rope out of the builder's hand. He broke out of his traces, dumping the stone several miles away. Svadilfaeri chased after the mare until they both disappeared over the horizon.

Unable to find the horses after chasing them for several hours, the builder returned to begin the arduous task of carrying the heavy stones by himself. He labored feverishly all that day and the next, running back and forth with stones, chiseling out and laying course after course of blocks. He worked all night without a rest, but when the sun rose on the first day of summer, the wall was still several blocks short.

And all the gods except for Loki were there to witness his failure. The builder had worked for months creating this incredible fortress, all for nothing. He flew into a rage, throwing stones and tools every which way. As he lost control, he dropped all pretense of disguise and revealed that he had been a mountain-giant all along. Odin immediately declared their oaths of nonviolence null and void, and he called for Thor. The god of thunder came like a bolt of lightning, driving in from halfway around the world in his chariot drawn by terrifying goats. Thor paid the builder's fee, but not what he was hoping for: He brought the mighty hammer Mjolnir down on the giant's head, crushing his skull and sending him down, down, down even below Niflheim.

Some time later, Loki gave birth to a gray, eight-legged foal. He thought it best to give it to Odin to smooth things out between them. And that's how the gods got the walls of Asgard repaired and Odin ended up with Sleipnir, the best horse ever in all the nine worlds.

Loki's Dangerous Children

There was a certain giantess Loki liked to visit from time to time. Her name was Angrboda, and she lived in the dark forest of Ironwood to the east of Midgard, in Jotunheim. Before long she presented Loki with three children: Jormungand (soon to be called the Midgard Serpent), Fenrir the wolf, and a wicked little girl named Hel, whose face was half deathly pale and half black as pitch.

When the Aesir learned of these strange children, they consulted oracles and seers to try to discover what their arrival might mean. All the omens they found pointed to the great evil that could be expected from the siblings. They would bring only misery and pain into the world.

Odin commanded that they be brought before him so he could judge for himself. One look was all it took: He saw the death and destruction in their future. He would have had them all killed right there, but that would have desecrated the holy place where they stood. Instead, he lifted up Jormungand (still quite small) and flung him into the ocean encircling the world; there the serpent grew and grew until eventually it could bite its own tail. He sent Hel down into Niflheim to look after all the dead from the nine worlds. She would be responsible for housing all those who died from disease or old age, plus those depraved souls thought to be worthy of punishment in the afterlife. Coming up with ways to torment liars and murderers seemed a good way to keep her occupied. When Loki and Angrboda's

Hel and Garm

other son, the monstrous hound Garm, was born, they sent him directly to Hel to be her watchdog.

But Odin decided that Fenrir should stay in Asgard, where they could keep an eye on him. All the gods except Tyr were terrified to go near the wolf; he alone had the courage to bring him food. But when they saw how quickly Fenrir was growing, the gods knew he couldn't be allowed to roam free much longer. They forged strong iron chains and suggested to Fenrir that he try his strength against them. Being young and arrogant, he agreed. Tyr wrapped the chains around the wolf's legs and locked them, but with one kick Fenrir broke the chains and scattered the fragments.

The gods forged a second chain, twice as strong. This took a while, and in the meantime Fenrir grew even bigger and a bit wiser. When the gods tempted him to try the new chains by saying how much fame he'd gain if he broke them, Fenrir took the time to consider whether it was a good idea. But then he did it anyway. He had to strain a little harder this time, but in the end he burst the chains and sent the pieces flying.

Finally Odin realized that ordinary chains, no matter how strong, would never hold the beast. He sent Skirnir, Frey's messenger, down into the world of the dark-elves to have the dwarfs make a chain that couldn't be broken. After what seemed like ages, the dwarfs presented Skirnir with long, silken ribbon, very soft and delicate to the touch.

"You have to be joking!" said Skirnir. "Something this weak will never hold the wolf!"

"Just try and break it," said a dwarf.

Skirnir found that the ribbon was much stronger than it looked. However hard he pulled, he couldn't tear it or even stretch it.

"What's it made of?" he asked.

"Six very special ingredients," said a dwarf. "The sound of a cat's footstep, a woman's beard, a mountain's roots, the sinews of a bear, a fish's breath, and a bird's spit."

That sounded ridiculous to Skirnir, but he couldn't argue with the results. He journeyed back up to Asgard and showed the ribbon to the gods. He told them it was called Gleipnir. Thor tested it himself and declared it worth a try.

The gods brought Fenrir to an island on a lake and invited him to try his strength against this new fetter—it could hardly be called a chain. But Fenrir was fully grown now, and he was very suspicious.

"It looks pretty weak to me," said Fenrir, "but if that's the case, then I won't win any fame by breaking it. On the other hand, if it was made by magic to be unbreakable, then I'd be a fool to let you tie it around my legs."

"Consider this," said Odin. "Since you had no trouble with the iron chains, this should be no problem. However, if it happens that you can't break it, we'll see that you're not a threat to us, and we'll set you free."

"Ha! I bet!" roared Fenrir. "You promise to set me free? Fine. Let one of you put his hand in my mouth as a mark of that promise."

The gods looked at one another, and it seemed as if none of them would offer to do it until Tyr stepped forward. He put his right hand into the wolf's mouth. The gods tied the ribbon securely around Fenrir's legs, and he immediately began to struggle. But the more he struggled, the tighter and stronger the ribbon became. He knew he was caught, so he crunched down and bit off Tyr's hand.

The gods attached a cord to the fetter, threaded the cord through an enormous stone slab, and sank the slab deep beneath the earth. They rolled a boulder on top to keep it all in place. All the while, Fenrir snapped at them with his knife-like teeth. The gods jammed a sword into his mouth with the hope that he wouldn't be able to bite anyone ever again. The drool that flowed from his perpetually open mouth became the River Van, also called "Hope."

And there Fenrir will lie, it is said, until the coming of Ragnarok, when he will be set free. That's the day that Odin fears most.

Loki's Head Wager

After the Aesir-Vanir War had ended but before the gods had found a way of getting the walls of Asgard rebuilt, Thor awoke one day to discover that his wife was bald. Sif had always had the longest, most beautiful golden-blond tresses of any of the goddesses, and so it was a shock to see her head as round and bare as an egg. Thor's gasp was enough to wake her. Despite his pleading for her not to, Sif picked up a mirror and saw the damage for herself. She was inconsolable.

Thor wasn't known for his quick thinking, but even he knew who the culprit had to be. He tore out of his hall in a flash and headed toward Idavoll in the middle of Asgard. He didn't need to go far before he noticed a group of elves and godlings laughing at something in their midst. When he got closer, he saw that it was Loki, prancing around in a blond wig and striking suggestive poses. With a yell, Thor grabbed Loki around his throat and squeezed. His rage made his speech a bit garbled, but the part about breaking every bone in Loki's body was clear enough.

"Just a (gasp) joke. I'll (gasp) fix it. I (gasp) swear," gurgled Loki as he tried to loosen Thor's iron grip.

"How?" Thor asked. He allowed Loki a gulp of air.

"You should know I would never have done such a thing in the first place unless I knew I could make it right," said Loki. "In fact, I guarantee her hair will be even better than before."

"Not possible."

"Oh, but it is, my dear Thor. It is," said Loki. "Down in the world of the dark-elves there are metalsmiths of tremendous skill and unusual cunning. They can make hair for her that's even more beautiful." Thor was understandably skeptical, but with assurances that Loki wouldn't come back to Asgard unless he had a solution, Thor let him go.

Loki ran down the Bifrost to Midgard, then through murky caves far below the earth. Eventually he reached the world of the dark-elves, where he searched out a pair of dwarfs, the sons of Ivaldi, renowned for their uncanny skill in crafting. After a bit of haggling over a sum of gems as payment, they agreed to make not only magical gold hair, but also a special ship and a spear. (Loki knew he'd have to satisfy more than Sif to get back in the gods' good graces.)

When he'd taken delivery of these items and was preparing to head back to the world above, Loki heard chuckling behind him. A particularly ugly dwarf named Brokk stood there grinning and shaking his head. "If you have something to say, dwarf, say it quickly and crawl back under your rock," said Loki.

"I heard what you did to Sif. The roar of Thor's thunder reached us even here," said Brokk. "If you think you'll placate him with such pitiful gifts, you're even stupider than you look."

"Oh, I suppose you could do better," said Loki, seething with anger at having both his looks and his intelligence insulted in the same breath, but careful to keep a civil tongue since he was far from home.

"Not I. My brother. He could easily make three items better than those."

"How nice for him. Well, I have nothing left to pay him for his obviously fabulous talents, so this conversation is a waste of my valuable time," said Loki, turning to leave.

"Oh, Eitri would do it for free," said Brokk.

"Free?" Loki stopped in mid-turn.

"If they don't surpass the items constructed by the sons of Ivaldi, you pay nothing."

"And if they do?" asked Loki.

Sif and her golden hair

"You simply pay with your head," said Brokk with an evil grin. "I'll even let the gods be the judges. How much more fair could it be?"

"Done!" said Loki before he'd stopped to think the whole thing through.

Brokk went to his brother's workshop and told Eitri about the wager. Eitri wasn't thrilled about being mixed up in the affairs of gods, but he agreed to do it if Brokk provided the muscle to work the enormous magical forge. First Eitri placed a pig's hide in the forge. He told Brokk to work the bellows and not to stop for any reason, then Eitri left for a while. As Brokk pumped, a fly flew onto his arm and bit him repeatedly, but the dwarf didn't miss a beat. Finally Eitri returned and pulled a large boar from the forge, its bristles made of pure gold.

Next Eitri put several gold ingots into the forge and told Brokk to pump the bellows once more. Eitri left, and again a fly bit Brokk—this time on his neck, again and again, even harder than before. But Brokk didn't stop, and when Eitri came back, he pulled a beautiful gold ring out of the forge.

Finally Eitri dumped in a huge load of iron, gave Brokk the same instructions, and left. This time the fly went straight for his face, munching on his eyelids. Brokk fought hard to concentrate, but as blood ran into his eyes he just couldn't stand it anymore. He swatted the fly. Eitri was furious when he returned, certain that Brokk had ruined his creation. But when he pulled out a massive hammer, he was satisfied that it had turned out even better than he'd imagined—even if the handle was a little short.

Loki and Brokk made the arduous climb back to Asgard, and Odin called an assembly of the gods to settle the wager. Loki presented his gifts first. To Odin, he gave the spear called Gungnir, explaining that nothing could stop its thrust. Odin, the All-Father, seemed favorably impressed, but sometimes it was hard to tell with him. Next he gave Sif the golden hair, along with many apologies. The shimmering strands attached themselves painlessly to her scalp, and she was overjoyed. Loki breathed a sigh of relief, but he knew he wasn't safe yet.

Lastly, he took a folded square of cloth from his pocket and tossed it into the center of the hall. It unfolded into a gigantic ship! The gods were amazed as Loki explained that this ship—called *Skidbladnir*—could carry all of them, with all their war gear, and that it would always have a strong breeze behind it. He folded the magical ship back up and gave it to the god Frey, hoping to get the Vanir gods on his side.

Then it was Brokk's turn. He bowed and presented Odin with Draupnir, the golden arm-ring with the power to drip eight more gold rings, just as big, every nine days. Odin almost broke into a smile. Brokk then gave the boar to Frey. He said it was called Gullinbursti; it could run across sky and sea faster than any horse, and the light shining from its bristles would make even Niflheim as bright as day. Finally he brought out the hammer, Mjolnir, and gave it to Thor. The dwarf explained that Thor could hit as hard as he liked with this hammer and it would never break, it would always hit its target when thrown, and it would always return to his hand. Furthermore, it was small enough to hide in his shirt. Thor's grin was unmistakable.

Much to Loki's dismay, the gods quickly came to the unanimous decision that Brokk was the winner. Mjolnir was simply the best defense against giants, making it the most valuable of the precious items. Brokk turned to Loki. "Time to collect," he said. "If you can catch me!" said Loki, and he sped away in his shoes that let him run over sea and sky. Thor was after him in a second. He caught up with him near Valhalla and dragged him back. Brokk approached with a knife in his hand and a gleam in his eye.

"Wait!" pleaded Loki, "I wagered my head, but not my neck! It's not yours to touch!"

A murmur of agreement ran through the assembled gods, and Brokk knew he wouldn't get what he'd come for. But he had an idea. "Hold him, please," he said. As Thor held Loki down, Brokk tried to pierce his lips, but his knife wouldn't penetrate the divine skin.

"Hmmm. If only my brother, Awl, was here," said Brokk. In the blink of an eye, an awl with the sharpest point ever was in his hand. He pierced holes in Loki's lips and sewed them up tight with a narrow strip of leather.

And that's how the gods got some of their most prized possessions—and how they got Loki to shut up, at least for a little while.

Thor the Bride

The first thing Thor did every morning (after checking to see that his wife's hair was still there) was to reach for his hammer, Mjolnir. One morning it was nowhere to be found. Thor fumbled about in the bed and on the floor looking for it, and he began to shake with rage when he realized that it was really missing.

"LOKI!" Thor bellowed, loud enough to be heard across Asgard.

For once, Thor didn't have to go looking for the trickster. Loki ran to Thor's hall, curious to see what had made the god of thunder so angry. He hoped it was something good.

"Where's my hammer?" Thor yelled at Loki.

"I didn't take it! I don't have it! I swear by Odin's beard!" screamed Loki, frantically backing up. Thor looked Loki in the eye to see if he was lying, but it was impossible to tell. That just made Thor more frustrated.

"Look, I'll help you find your hammer," said Loki, "and I know exactly where to start."

Together they walked over into Folkvang, to the beautiful hall Sessrumnir. Inside, countless warriors sat feasting. Some had horrible wounds but didn't seem to mind them as they enjoyed good food, drink, and fellowship. At the head of the hall sat Freyja, the goddess of love, petting one of her large cats. Loki and Thor explained what had brought them to her hall.

"And so, if we could borrow your falcon cloak to go look for Mjolnir, we'd be most appreciative," said Loki.

"If it were made of pure gold and silver, I'd still lend it for such a mission," said Freyja. "None of us is safe while Mjolnir is missing." She handed over the cloak, and soon Loki was flying in the shape of a falcon out over the world, searching far and wide. It occurred to him that those who stood to gain the most from Thor's losing his hammer were the giants, so he headed to Jotunheim. In a mountainous region called Thrymheim he came upon King Thrym sitting on a mound, braiding golden collars for his fierce hounds and brushing his magnificent horses.

"What so troubles the gods and elves that you've come all the way to Jotunheim, Loki?" asked the giant, seeing through the falcon disguise.

"Oh, I was just wondering if you might've seen Thor's hammer recently," said Loki.

"Seen it? I took it!" said Thrym, and he roared with laughter. "I won't tell you how I did it, but I will tell you that it's 24 miles below the earth, and the only way he's getting it back is if Freyja agrees to be my loving bride."

Loki winged his way back to Asgard and told Thor and Freyja about Thrym's demand. She didn't take the news well. In fact, she flew into such a rage that her shining necklace, Brisingamen, burst into pieces.

"Why are you so intent on marrying me off to a giant, Loki?" she shrieked. "You've called me boy-crazy in the past, but I'd have to be completely insane to give myself to one of those ugly brutes! Get out, both of you!"

While she calmed down, Thor and Loki got Odin to call an assembly of the gods to decide what should be done. A suggestion came from an unlikely source. Normally serious and quiet, Heimdall stepped forward and said, "We need to dress up Thor as Freyja, with a bridal veil over his head, Brisingamen around his neck, and a wife's house keys dangling from his waist."

"That sounds like something I'd think up," said Loki. "In other words, it's absolutely brilliant!"

"Now, wait just a minute," said Thor. "There's no way I'm putting on a dress! I'd be the laughingstock of all the gods! That might be fine for you, Loki, but I—"

"Would you rather have giants living where Asgard once stood?" asked Loki.

So they dressed Thor up as Heimdall had suggested, adding some padding to give him a woman's figure. They made sure that the bridal linens were loose enough to hide his muscles and that the veil covered his beard. Brisingamen was repaired and hung around his neck to complete the disguise. Loki transformed himself into a handmaiden, and they set off in the goat-drawn chariot for Thrymheim.

When they arrived, a celebration was waiting for them. Benches were set up for the hulking guests, and decorations hung from all the trees. Slaughtered oxen and dozens of salmon were roasting over blazing fires. The giants jockeyed for position to catch a glimpse of the ravishing Freyja. Loki led Thor (who tried to take dainty steps) up to Thrym's throne.

"Your Majesty," said Loki the handmaiden, "I present to you the lovely Freyja, daughter of Njord of Noatun."

Thrym's greedy, lustful eyes drank in "her" form. "I have black cattle with golden horns that are the envy of all the giants. I have more arm rings of gold and silver than I can count. Freyja was the only treasure I was missing, until today," he said. "Let the wedding feast begin!"

Much to Loki's horror, when the food was brought out Thor immediately gobbled up an ox, stripped eight salmon down to the bone, and downed three horns of mead. Thrym was amazed. "I've never seen a bride—even a giant bride—eat and drink that much at one sitting," he said.

Loki was quick with an answer. "Oh, the Lady Freyja is simply famished. She hasn't eaten for eight days because she was so excited to come to Jotunheim."

Thrym could only say, "Hmmm." But finally the giant king could hold back no longer. He lifted up the veil to give his bride a kiss, and what he saw made him gasp and step back in fear.

"Her eyes! They burn like twin flames! Does she hate me so?" asked Thrym.

"Hate? No, it's *love*, Your Majesty," explained Loki. "Freyja's eyes are bloodshot because hasn't slept for eight nights. She stayed awake thinking of nothing but her future husband."

Just then an old crone of a giantess approached. "If you want my friendship and love here in your new home, my dear, you'd be wise to make me a gift of your gold rings," she said to "Freyja." Thor wasn't sure what to do. He didn't want to reveal

Thor gets revenge on Thrym the giant

his massive hands, hidden in the folds of his dress, and he didn't want to speak and give the game away.

Thrym stepped in, however. "Before Freyja gives up her bridal gifts to you or me," he said, "our union should be blessed. Bring out the hammer!"

Thor's ears pricked up. Of course, Mjolnir was considered a powerful and holy object even to the giants! He trembled with joy as the hammer was paraded out and placed right in his lap. With a hearty laugh that no one could mistake for a woman's, Thor snatched up Mjolnir and smashed in Thrym's head. As for the crone, instead of a golden ring she got a hammer blow that sent her down to Niflheim. Grinning from ear to ear, Thor made quick work of the rest of the wedding guests.

Thor wore that dress all the way back to Asgard. But he didn't notice or care—he had his hammer back.

Of Apples and Nuptials

One day, three of the Aesir—Odin, Loki, and Hoenir—set out to see the world. They trekked through dark forests, over craggy mountains, and across desolate wastes. For several days they'd been traveling in an area where there was very little to eat, so they were relieved when they came upon a herd of oxen. They slaughtered one and put it in an oven they'd dug out of the ground, with hot stones in the bottom. They covered it all up with grassy turf and waited for the ox to cook. After several hours, thinking the meat had to be done, they opened the oven—but found that the meat was still raw. They heated more stones and tried again, only to get the same result. The ox wouldn't cook, and the gods were stumped.

"Perhaps if you agreed to share, I'd allow the oven to cook the ox," said a voice above their heads. The three looked up and saw an eagle perched in the branches of an oak tree. The eagle was even bigger than the ox. Odin said the eagle was welcome to eat his fill if he could do what he said.

The eagle swooped down, tore open the oven, and promptly scarfed down all four ox legs. Loki was livid. He cracked off a large branch of the tree and swung it at the bird with all his might. But the eagle caught the branch in his talons and took off —and Loki found himself unable to let go! The eagle soared high, nearly pulling Loki's arms out of their sockets. Then he dove down and skimmed along the ground, dragging Loki over sharp rocks and prickly bushes until he was bruised and bloody and his clothes were in rags.

"Stop!" screamed Loki. "I'll do anything you want! Just let me go!"

The eagle hovered in midair. "Anything?" he asked.

"Anything. I swear," answered Loki.

Loki walked back into camp to find Odin and Hoenir feasting on the roasted ox. He joined them and entertained them late into the night with the thrilling story of how he'd managed to break free and escape from the eagle. The next morning, the three gods headed back to Asgard.

Some time later, Loki took a walk one morning to Idunn's grove, where she was picking apples. These were the apples of everlasting youth that the gods ate to keep old age at bay.

"Good morning to you, Idunn," said Loki. "It looks like you have a fine crop of apples there."

"They are indeed," said Idunn.

"Do you ever worry that you'll run out?" asked Loki.

"My trees have always produced what we've needed," answered Idunn, slightly annoyed at being interrupted in her work, but even more annoyed at the suggestion that she'd let the apple supply run out.

"Oh, absolutely, absolutely. But gods being what they are, our numbers do seem to increase over time, wouldn't you agree?" That gave Idunn something to think about. Loki continued, "It's just that I noticed some apples growing outside of Asgard that looked as delicious as yours. Maybe even more delicious."

"Where are these apples?" she asked.

"I could show you right now, if you like," said Loki, "You should bring your box of apples with you, to compare."

Idunn agreed to go with him as soon as she was done picking. Soon they were hiking in the countryside beyond the walls of Asgard. "How much farther, Loki?" asked Idunn.

"It won't be long now," said Loki. Just then, a mountain-giant ran out of the woods, grabbed Idunn and her apples, transformed into an eagle, and flew off. Loki returned home by a roundabout way and pretended that nothing was amiss. Very soon, however, the gods began to notice Idunn's disappearance. Not only was her husband, Bragi, overcome with worry, but the absence of her apples was felt. The gods were getting gray, and creases were appearing on their faces. Odin called for an assembly to deal with this increasingly grave matter.

All were gathered except for the guardian Heimdall, and they wondered where he might be. Shortly, however, the White God came shuffling into Gladsheim, leaning heavily on a staff. He was bent and haggard. "Sorry for the delay," said Heimdall. "The distance from Himinbjorg seems longer than it once did. I have information that will be of interest—"

"Heimdall, you look exhausted," interrupted Loki. "Please come with me, and we'll find a place where you can nap."

"I'm not interested in going anyplace you want to take me," said Heimdall, resisting Loki's attempts to grab his arm. "I saw Idunn leave Asgard with you the day she disappeared."

The gods were furious. Thor and Bragi held Loki as Odin tore into him with words, telling him exactly how sorry he'd be if he didn't get Idunn back. Loki blurted out the story of how the eagle was really a mountain-giant and that it had nearly killed him, only letting him go when he promised to lure Idunn outside. He had no idea where she might be.

"That eagle, eh?" muttered Odin. "Hold him here. I'll be right back."

Odin went to look out over the worlds from his throne, Hlidskjalf. He returned a short while later. "His name is Thjatsi, and he has her in his stronghold in Thrymheim. Loki will go alone using Freyja's falcon cape," said Odin.

"You trust me to just fly out of here by myself?" asked Loki, amazed.

"No, but I trust we could find you wherever you might try to hide," answered Odin.

Soon Loki was flying far from Asgard in the shape of a falcon, heading to the snowy peaks of Thrymheim in the land of the giants. Below him he saw a lake. Thjatsi, the giant, was out fishing in a boat. Loki made a beeline for the giant's fortress and found Idunn sitting glumly in the highest tower. He landed next to her on the bed.

"Cheer up, Idunn! I'm here to rescue you," he said.

"Loki? Is that you?" she asked, her anger quickly growing stronger than her surprise. "When I get my hands on you—" but Idunn never got to finish her sentence, because Loki turned her and her box of apples into a nut and snatched it up in his talons.

As Loki flew toward home over the lake, Thjatsi spotted him. The giant turned into an eagle once more and chased after Loki. No matter how Loki turned, banked, and dove—over, under, around, and through the clouds—he couldn't shake the eagle. Thjatsi stayed hot on his tail all the way back to heaven.

Heimdall looked out from the battlements of Asgard and saw the falcon approaching with the nut. He also saw the giant eagle in hot pursuit. He blew his horn, and the gods ran out to see what was going on—well, as fast as they could run, seeing as they were all quite old now. Odin knew exactly what to do. He had everyone gather all the kindling they could find and stack it against the walls. The god of war Tyr and the silent god Vidar, son of Odin, stood by with torches. As the falcon got close, Odin waved him in. Loki flew over the wall of Asgard, and at Odin's signal Tyr and Vidar set fire to the kindling. Thjatsi couldn't stop himself, and he flew right through the wall of flames. The fire burned off all his feathers, and he crashed inside the gates of Asgard. Despite their weakened state, the gods managed to kill the giant.

Idunn returned to normal, and with her apples back, so did the rest of the gods. Loki wasn't welcome in many halls after that. But the story doesn't end there. Not many days later, a loud banging at the gates woke up all of Asgard.

"Open up, puny Aesir! You have a blood-debt to pay, and I'm here to collect!" roared a female voice.

The gods gathered on the battlements and saw that it was a giantess in full armor, outfitted with many weapons. Before they could even ask what she wanted, she shouted, "I'm Skadi, the daughter of Thjatsi. You owe me compensation for my father's death, or I'll take one of your heads as payment!"

Thor was already whirling Mjolnir over his head, but Odin stopped him. He wasn't ready for more bloodshed at their gates just yet, and he knew there had to be another solution.

"Send your son, Forseti, down to talk with her," Odin said to his son, Baldr. "He always knows how to get people to compromise."

Baldr did as he asked, and Forseti exited the gates and started negotiations with Skadi. The gods watched as they talked all day. Skadi shouted a few times and even threatened Forseti with her spear, but he remained calm. Toward evening, he walked back inside and announced the agreement they'd reached.

"She says she'll be satisfied if we do two things: one, let her choose one of us as her husband; and two, make her laugh," said Forseti. The gods moaned. No one wanted to marry her, and no one thought they could ever make this scowling giantess laugh. "At least I got her to agree that she had to choose her husband by his feet," Forseti added. So they strung up a cloth, and the male gods stood behind it with just their bare feet showing. Skadi walked down the line, trying to guess which feet belonged to Baldr, because he was the handsomest of all. She spotted a pair that weren't only handsome in form but had skin that was fair and smooth. They had to be Baldr's.

But when they pulled back the cloth, there was Njord, the god of wind, waves, and fire. Walking on the sand and in the crashing surf evidently had given him great feet. She was disappointed, and so was he.

Given her mood just then, making her laugh seemed an impossible task. But Loki knew he had to try, since he was getting blamed for all this. He tied a string around the neck of a nanny goat, and the other end he tied around his…well, testicles. Then he and the goat proceeded to fight a tug of war. Back and forth they pulled, both of them bleating pitifully. Even the most somber gods were chuckling, but Skadi managed to keep a straight face. Finally the string snapped, and Loki fell with a howl right into Skadi's lap. The way he grabbed his privates and his look of anguish broke her. She laughed long and loud, and it sounded a lot like the braying of a donkey.

As an added bit of compensation, Odin tossed Thjatsi's eyes into the night sky, where they would shine like two stars for the rest of time.

When Skadi and Njord were married, neither of them wanted to live where the other did. He loved the sea, and she loved the mountains. He loved sailing, and she loved skiing. They decided to split their time, spending nine days at one place and then nine days at the other. He complained about the howling wolves, and she complained about the screeching seagulls. Neither of them was very happy about the situation, but an agreement was an agreement.

Otter's Ransom, Sigurd, and the Cursed Treasure

One time when Odin, Loki, and Hoenir went out to explore the world, one simple act turned into tragedy for generations to come. They had been walking for days when they came to a river and decided to rest. As they sat there talking, a very large otter carrying a very large salmon climbed out of the water and lay down on the bank to enjoy its catch. Loki, always one to see an opportunity, picked up a rock and threw it at the otter's head, killing him instantly.

"Ha! An otter and a salmon with one throw!" he cried, and he dashed down to collect his prizes. They skinned the otter and roasted the salmon for lunch. Then they continued on their journey.

Just before dark, they arrived at a farmhouse. The owner, a big man named Hreidmar, answered the door and invited them into the hall. The gods asked if they could spend the night, and they offered the otter skin as payment. Hreidmar took the skin and examined it closely.

"I should show this to my sons," he said. "Fafnir! Regin! Come here! We have guests!"

Two muscular youths came and saw what their father was holding. They looked shocked.

"Yes, your brother Otr is dead," said Hreidmar, "and these men are responsible."

Before the gods could reach for their weapons, the father and his two sons grabbed them and tied them up with unusually strong rope. Although they looked like simple farmers, they were in fact powerful magical beings.

"You'll pay with your lives for what you've done," said Hreidmar.

"How about gold?" asked Loki. "Name your price, and it will be a ransom for our lives. It was all an accident, after all." Hreidmar was greedy, so that solution appealed to him. "Fair enough. First you must fill his skin with gold, then stand it up in this room. When you've covered the skin completely with gold, we'll call the debt paid."

The gods agreed, and immediately Loki set off to get the gold. He borrowed a fishnet from the goddess Ran and dashed deep down below the earth, where the dark-elves and dwarfs lived. There in a black underground lake, a rich dwarf named Andvari often hunted for food in the depths while he took the shape of a big fish called a pike. Loki waited for him to swim by and threw the net over him.

"If you want to live, dwarf, you'll give me all your gold," said Loki.

Andvari gave in and led Loki to the cave where he kept his gold. After Loki had gathered it all up in a huge bag, he caught sight of something shiny peeking out under Andvari's arm. "What's that?" he bellowed. "Holding out on me, eh? Give it here, right now!"

Andvari showed him the gold arm-ring, but he pleaded to keep it. "Leave me this, please," Andvari said. "It's just one ring, but it has the power to grow my gold back."

"Not a chance," Loki said, snatching the ring away.

"Then I curse this ring and all the treasure!" screamed Andvari. "It will be the death of whoever owns it!"

"Glad to hear it!" laughed Loki, and he sped away.

Loki returned to Hreidmar's home and showed Odin the gold. Odin was especially in love with the ring and its power, and he hid it in his clothing. The gods filled the otter skin, stood it up, and piled gold over it. Hreidmar inspected their work and pointed out that one whisker was still showing. Sad that he had to do it, Odin took out the ring—called Andvaranaut, "Andvari's Gift"—and covered up the last whisker.

"So, do you accept our payment?" asked Loki.

"Yes," said Hreidmar, and he let them have their weapons and magical items back.

"Good," said Loki. "Now I can tell you that this treasure is cursed, and it will surely be the death of you!" Loki cackled and took to the sky with his magical shoes. Odin and Hoenir quickly made their exit and headed on foot back to Asgard.

Hreidmar was upset by Loki's words, but the power of the gold and the ring soon overcame that feeling. He could think of nothing but his newfound wealth. Regin and Fafnir asked if they could have a share of the treasure; after all, Otr had been their brother. Hreidmar angrily told them that they would get nothing; the gold was all his.

The brothers waited until their father was asleep, then murdered him. But Fafnir turned on Regin. He put on Hreidmar's Helm of Terror and warned his brother to stay away or he'd kill him. Regin fled, and Fafnir took the treasure and placed it in a lair on Gnita Heath. There he lay down on the gold and let greed flow through him. He transformed himself into a fierce dragon so that no one would dare touch his treasure.

But Odin never forgot about that magical ring called Andvaranaut, and he plotted a way to get it back. He needed a hero.

***

The hall of King Volsung of Hunland had an unusual feature: it had been built around a living tree. One night a stranger entered during a feast. He was an old man and wore a hood that hid his face, but it was plain that he was missing an eye.

(This, of course, was Odin in one of his many disguises.) The old man carried a magnificent sword, and to everyone's surprise, he jammed it into the tree.

"Whoever pulls this sword from the tree will receive a great gift from me," croaked the old man, "and he'll receive an excellent sword, besides." And with that, he vanished.

Many warriors and great noblemen tried to pull the sword free, but none of them could budge it. But Sigmund, the king's son, easily pulled it loose. Many men envied him, but by the end of his life Sigmund would be hard pressed to say what, exactly, was the "great gift" he had received. First his father and brothers were murdered, and Sigmund had to go live in the forest with his first son. They put on wolfskins and became werewolves to prey on travelers. Sigmund later married, but his new wife poisoned his son, so he divorced her.

He married again, this time a princess named Hjordis, but a rival ambushed him with an army. It became clear that either Odin had been playing with him all along, or the All-Father had decided Sigmund just wasn't his chosen hero. A one-eyed man appeared on the battlefield, and Sigmund shattered his sword, Gram, against the man's spear. Before he died, he was able to give the shards of his sword to Hjordis.

Pregnant with Sigmund's child, Hjordis fled the country. She found refuge with Alf, the son of King Hjalprek, who fell in love with her and married her. When her son, Sigurd, was old enough, they sent him to be raised and trained by a foster father (a common practice for royalty in those days). This turned out to be none other than our old friend Regin, who had taken a job as a blacksmith at the king's court. He saw in the boy a hope for revenge and a way to get at his dragon-brother's treasure.

Regin taught Sigurd sports, chess, and several languages; but most importantly, he taught him how to fight. Day and night they trained, until Sigurd was stronger and more skillful than any warrior in the king's guard. Regin told Sigurd that he needed a good horse and should ask his stepfather for one. Alf generously let Sigurd choose any horse in his herd. A strange, one-eyed man standing nearby pointed out a beautiful gray steed. "That one's descended from Sleipnir, Odin's horse," he said. Before Sigurd could ask how he knew that, the man had disappeared. Sigurd took the horse and named it Grani.

Finally Regin felt that Sigurd was ready to go up against his brother Fafnir—now a dragon. He told the boy about Otr's ransom and how Fafnir had killed their father to get the treasure. (He left out his role in his father's death, as well as the part about the curse.) What Sigurd needed, however, was a sword, and he asked Regin to make him one. Regin used all his skill to forge a sword, but when Sigurd struck it against Regin's anvil to test it, it snapped in half. Regin forged another, with the same result. Finally Sigurd went to his mother and asked for the shards of Gram, his father's sword. She gladly gave them to him, thinking that he wanted to be a great warrior and not knowing about his plan to fight a dragon. Regin forged the shards into a new blade, and flames leaped from its edges as he pulled it from the fire. When Sigurd tested its strength, the sword split the anvil in half. To test its sharpness, he placed it point down in a river and then dropped a tuft of wool into the

Sigurd slays fafnir the dragon

water upstream. When the wool drifted up against the blade, Gram parted it easily. Sigurd had what he needed.

Regin and Sigurd rode to Gnita Heath, and Regin showed Sigurd the path the dragon took from its lair to the local river. The enormous footprints surprised Sigurd.

"You said he was just a serpent," he said.

"If you don't have the courage, we can just forget about this," snapped Regin. "But if you decide to do it, you should dig a trench in the path and lie there until he crawls over you, then stab him in the heart."

Regin rode away, and Sigurd was digging a trench when an old man with a long beard—Odin again—approached and asked what he was doing. When Sigurd told him, the old man said, "That's a terrible idea. The dragon's blood will run into the trench and burn you alive. Better to dig several trenches to direct the blood away from you."

Sigurd did as the man suggested. As he lay in his trench, he was calm and unafraid, awaiting what was about to happen. It started with a rumble, growing to a deafening thunder that shook the ground. The blackness of the dragon's bulk passed mere inches above him, and Sigurd almost felt like he was in his own grave. He stabbed his sword upward, and it slid easily between the beast's scales into its heart. Fafnir the dragon thrashed about in agony, uprooting trees with his tail and head, while blood poured from him. He breathed venom all around him while bellowing out his death roars. Sigurd stayed in his trench until the dragon was still; when he stood up, he saw that all the other trenches were filled with fiery blood and poison.

"It was my brother who sent you, wasn't it?" whispered the dragon. "What's your name?"

Sigurd didn't want to tell, knowing full well the power a dying curse can have.

"No matter. He'll surely cause your death, as he's caused mine," said Fafnir, and he died.

Regin rejoined Sigurd. He looked sorrowful and voiced regret at the death of his brother. This led Sigurd to look at him with suspicion. "You ran away pretty quickly when there was work to be done," he said.

"And you couldn't have done it without the sword I made for you," said Regin. "Now do me a favor. Cut out his heart and roast it for me."

While Sigurd did as his foster father asked, Regin went to take a nap. When some of the juice foamed out from the heart, Sigurd touched it to test if it was done. It burned, and he stuck his finger in his mouth. When the dragon's heart-blood touched his tongue, he felt as though he'd just woken up.

"There sits poor Sigurd," said a voice above his head. "He's dumber than I thought, if he leaves Regin alive after killing his brother."

"I know," said another voice, "he should kill Regin and take all the treasure for himself. He risked his life for it, after all."

"Not just that," said yet another voice, "he should eat that whole heart himself and get the wisdom it holds."

Sigurd looked up and realized that the nuthatches sitting in the branches over his head were talking—and he could understand every word! "If the birds can see it plain as day, I'm certainly not going to sit here and wait to be betrayed," he thought. He drew Gram for the second time that day and sliced Regin's head clean off. Both brothers were now gone, and Sigurd felt the world was better for it.

He went to Fafnir's cave and pulled open the iron doors. Inside was a mound of gold that nearly reached the ceiling—not just coins but also cups, jewelry, armor, and weapons of all kinds. The most precious things he found were the Helm of Terror, a golden suit of armor, a fine sword named Hrotti, and the magical ring Andvaranaut. He packed it all into sacks and loaded them onto Grani, who didn't mind the weight as long as it was Sigurd who was riding him.

***

Sigurd rode far away with his treasure. One day he came to a hill that seemed to be on fire. Riding closer, he saw a wall of flame-covered shields surrounding a golden-roofed hall. Inside the wall was someone in full armor lying on a slab, apparently asleep. He spurred Grani forward, and they leaped over the flames into the courtyard. Removing the helmet from the sleeping figure, Sigurd discovered that it was a woman. Her armor was so tight that it seemed to be biting into her flesh, so he cut it free. She awoke and said her name was Brynhild, and that she'd been a valkyrja before she angered Odin.

"He wanted a certain king to win a battle, but I gave the victory to the other side," she explained, "so Odin pricked me with a sleeping thorn—and there I lay until you found me."

Not only was she the most beautiful woman he'd ever seen, she was also the wisest, and she gave Sigurd many pieces of sage advice. They fell in love, and he stayed with her for several days. Before he left, Brynhild told him she was afraid they would never be together again. Sigurd brushed aside her fears and promised that they would be married. He gave her the ring Andvaranaut as a pledge of his love. Sigurd's fame as the slayer of the dragon Fafnir spread far and wide, and he was welcomed with great honors when he came to the court of King Gjuki. People were amazed at the fabulous treasure he carried. The king had three sons, Gunnar, Hogni, and Guttorm, and a daughter named Gudrun. The king's wife, Grimhild, thought that a rich, handsome prince like Sigurd would make a fine son-in-law. Being skilled in the magical arts, she brewed him a cup of mead of forgetfulness; when he drank it, he lost all memory of Brynhild. He fell in love with Gudrun, and they were soon married. At the marriage feast, Sigurd, Gunnar, and Hogni swore oaths of blood-brotherhood. Everyone was happy—but only for a very short time.

Gunnar soon decided that he needed a wife, too, and he set his sights on Brynhild. It was well known that she wouldn't marry any man who showed fear; to prove himself, he would have to jump over the flames that encircled her hall. But when he tried, his horse refused. Sigurd loaned him Grani, but Grani also refused. Knowing his horse would only jump for him, Sigurd suggested that he and Gunnar trade likenesses, using the magic Grimhild had taught them. Looking exactly like Gunnar, Sigurd spurred Grani forward and leaped over the flames. The earth shook and the flames rose higher, but through them went horse and rider. Brynhild couldn't help but be impressed, and although she was still waiting for Sigurd to return, she agreed to honor her oath and marry the man who had braved the flames.

Sigurd stayed three nights with Brynhild in the same bed, but he kept Gram unsheathed between them. When he left, he took Andvaranaut from her and gave her another ring from his hoard. Sigurd and Gunnar changed back to their original forms, and Gunnar took Brynhild home with him, overjoyed with his new bride.

Brynhild was shocked to find that Sigurd had married Gudrun and had no memory of her at all, but she tried to console herself with the fact that she was now married to a king. She even became friends with Gudrun, but jealousy simmered below the surface. One day Brynhild and Gudrun went to bathe in the Rhine River, and Brynhild decided to go upstream to put some distance between them.

"Why did you go all the way over there?" Gudrun asked.

"Well, you don't expect me to bathe in your dirty water, do you?" answered Brynhild. "After all, I'm the one married to a king who faced roaring flames to win me. Your husband will never inherit a throne."

"Sigurd slew a dragon, which is more than Gunnar will ever do," Gudrun shot back. "And it was Sigurd who had the courage to jump the flames and win you, not Gunnar! Look at what I'm wearing!"

Brynhild could see that Gudrun was wearing Andvaranaut, and her blood boiled with rage. After that, she thought of nothing but revenge for the humiliation she'd suffered. She fell into a fog of sadness, not leaving her room or eating. When Gunnar went to see what was bothering her, she told him about her conversation with Gudrun. She attacked Gunnar for his lack of courage and screamed that Sigurd had insulted them both by his actions. She couldn't go on the way things were. One of them—Brynhild, Gunnar, or Sigurd—needed to die.

Gunnar saw that there was only one way to make her happy again. He tried to convince his brother Hogni that they had to kill Sigurd, but Hogni reminded him that Sigurd was their blood-brother, and breaking their oath would make them untrust-worthy in everyone's eyes. Gunnar decided that their youngest brother, Guttorm, should do the deed. They told Guttorm that he'd get lots of gold and glory for killing Sigurd, and they gave him a magic potion to make him brave.

Guttorm crept in while Sigurd was sleeping and stabbed him through to the mattress. As Guttorm ran from the room, Sigurd grabbed his own sword and hurled it at his murderer, cutting him in two. And then Sigurd died.

While this was going on, Brynhild had Sigurd's three-year-old son killed. But the killings didn't end Brynhild's grief; in fact, they made it worse. Predicting that all their lives would end in blood and sorrow, she stabbed herself with a sword and threw herself onto Sigurd's funeral pyre.

Gudrun, too, was crushed by sadness after the death of her husband and son, but her crafty mother gave her the mead of forgetfulness. That dulled her grief, and she forgave her two surviving brothers. Grimhild then married Gudrun off to Atli, the mighty king of the Huns and the brother of Brynhild. Grimhild hoped for a strong ally to help their weakened kingdom. Gudrun had two sons with Atli, but she never loved him.

***

Years passed, and King Atli wondered where Sigurd's hoard of gold might be. He invited Gudrun's brothers to visit him, sending them gifts and promising them lands. Although Gudrun tried to warn Gunnar and Hogni that Atli was planning to betray them—and they had premonitions of their own—they decided to go anyway. But first the brothers hid their hoard of gold in the waters of the Rhine. They rowed to the land of the Huns with an army of many men—but Atli had an even bigger army there to greet them when they landed.

"You only need to hand over the gold that is rightfully Gudrun's," said Atli, "and then you may feast with us."

But Gunnar answered, "We will never give up the gold willingly, and you don't have the means to take it. The only feast you'll provide is one for the eagles and the wolves."

"So be it. I've plotted your deaths for a long time," said Atli.

"However long you planned this, it wasn't enough. You're not ready," said Hogni.

The two armies clashed in a hail of arrows that darkened the sky. Though their force was smaller, the two brothers advanced across the battlefield, hacking a bloody path through Atli's ranks. Watching from her window, Gudrun came to a decision: She put on a coat of mail, grabbed a sword, and joined her brothers in battle. Dozens of Atli's finest champions fell before them. But Gunnar's and Hogni's men were falling, too, and when the siblings entered the king's hall, they were the only ones of their army left alive. The Huns put the brothers in chains, and Atli sent Gudrun back to her rooms. The king questioned the brothers separately about the treasure, but neither would tell where it was hidden.

"I'd sooner see the bloody heart of my brother Hogni than reveal the location," said Gunnar. Very soon that was just what they showed him. Hogni had remained silent while they cut out his heart.

Gunnar only laughed, "Now I know the secret is safe with me. I'd rather let the Rhine keep the gold than see it on the arms of the Huns."

Atli had Gunnar thrown into a snake pit with his arms bound. Gudrun managed to get a harp to him, knowing his skill with that instrument. Using his toes, Gunnar played a lilting, sleepy melody, and the snakes fell asleep—all except for one large adder, which bit him on his heart and killed him.

Gudrun pretended to be reconciled with Atli, and they prepared an enormous funeral feast in honor of her two brothers and all the men who had died in battle. Vast amounts of wine were consumed, and the feast became boisterous.

"My sons!" called Atli. "Where are my sons? Why aren't they here?"

"Why, they are here, my king," said Gudrun. "Their skulls are the cups from which you are drinking wine mixed with their blood. Their hearts have been roasted, and you are eating them."

Horrified but too drunk to think clearly, Atli soon passed out. That night Gudrun and the son of her brother Hogni stabbed him repeatedly in his sleep. Gudrun then set the hall on fire, and the blaze killed all of Atli's remaining servants and warriors. Gudrun threw herself into the sea, hoping to drown, but she washed up on a distant shore, alive. Another king married her and they had several children—all of whom died violent deaths.

The lines of King Volsung and King Gjuki were no more. The curse of Andvari's gold had run its bloody course. And Odin never recovered Andvaranaut, either.

So—be careful where you throw rocks.

Frey's Courtship

Frey was curious about what visions came to Odin when he sat in his all-seeing throne, Hlidskjalf. One morning at dawn, when no one else was around, he snuck into Valaskjalf and climbed up into the high-seat. What he saw left him speechless. He watched a woman step out of a large, beautiful hall. She was the most breathtaking woman he'd ever seen, and when she raised her arms, light radiated from her to brighten all the worlds—or so it seemed to Frey.

Her name was Gerd, and he knew he had to have her. But what crushed his hopes was the fact that she was the daughter of the mountain-giants Gymir and Aurboda, and she lived in the peaks far to the north in the outer reaches of Jotunheim. A union was next to impossible.

Frey went home to Alfheim sadder than he'd ever been before. He refused to eat, sleep, or drink. He sent away all visitors. His father, Njord, and his stepmother, Skadi, grew concerned, and they sent for Frey's servant, Skirnir, to see if he could find out what was the matter.

"Fine. I'll check on him," said Skirnir, "but I don't expect a warm greeting."

Frey at first refused to speak to him, but Skirnir was insistent and got him to open up about Gerd and how lovesick he was. Frey told Skirnir, "You have to go to her and tell her how I feel. Bring her to me whether her father says yes or no. If I don't have her, I'll die! Do you understand?"

"Yes, yes, I do," said Skirnir, "but her home isn't simply a short walk away. It's a long journey filled with many dangers, not the least of which is the family of giants around her."

"You'll be well rewarded, I swear."

"I was hoping I could have my reward now, as it could be useful on the trip," said Skirnir. "I'm referring to your magical sword."

"The one that can fight on its own?" asked Frey.

"The very one."

"Yes, anything! Take it! Take my horse, too!" blurted Frey. "Just bring me Gerd!"

Skirnir strapped on the sword and left Frey's house. He mounted Frey's horse and rode hard over the Bifrost and into Jotunheim. A full six days he galloped through dark forests and frozen wastes, up into the high mountains. Finally he arrived at Gymir's fortress, but he found it surrounded by fire and ferocious-looking dogs. Skirnir jumped the flames, causing thunder to shake the fortress and setting the dogs to barking.

"What's that racket outside?" Gerd asked her handmaiden.

"There's a young man just getting off his horse. I think he wants to come inside," said the handmaiden.

"You'd better invite him in before my father comes," said Gerd.

When Skirnir entered, he bowed deeply. "I come bringing words of love from the god Frey. If you become his wife, I can give you apples of everlasting youth," said Skirnir.

"I won't become a slave for a few apples," said Gerd.

"For gold, then. All you ever desire," said Skirnir.

Gerd rolled her eyes. "I have all the gold I need here in my father's hall," she said.

"What if I were to threaten you with this sword? Would you declare your love for Frey then?"

"If you threaten me, my father will kill you. Make no mistake about it."

"But I might kill your father. What then? Would you let that happen?" said Skirnir. But Gerd was no longer listening to him, and he was running out of ideas. His only chance was his knowledge of rune magic.

"Look at the rune I've carved on this wand," said Skirnir. "With it I will curse you to sit out your lonely life on this mountain, growing ever older and uglier. Men will be frightened to look at you, and you will be forced to marry some hideous, three-headed giant. You'll have to serve his every whim in a dark, dank hovel below Niflheim, with nothing but spoiled goat's milk to drink. However, I can scratch the rune away as easily as I scratched it on. It's up to you."

Gerd thought about it, and she began to see her father's house as more of a prison than a home. "You've said enough. I never thought I'd marry one of the gods, but I suppose I will," she said.

"What should I tell Frey? When will you meet him?"

"Tell him that I'll meet him at Barey in nine days, and there we'll be married," said Gerd.

Delighted with his success, Skirnir hopped back on his horse and rode as fast as he could for six days, all the way back to Alfheim. He told Frey the good news, and the god was overjoyed. But then he fell back into a gloomy mood.

"I won't get to see her for another three whole days," he moaned. "One night is long, two nights are longer, but how can I stand to wait for three? I've known whole months that have gone by faster than this will seem."

But Frey somehow managed to wait for three whole days, and he and Gerd were married. Skirnir kept the sword as a reward for his matchmaking, and that was why Frey had to use an antler to kill the giant Beli. He would miss his sword even more when it came time to fight the fire-giant Surt at Ragnarok. But that's another story.

Thor's Journey to Utgard

One day Thor decided to go adventuring in the land of the giants, and Loki asked to go along with him. So they got into Thor's goat-drawn chariot and drove out of Asgard. At the end of the first day, near the border of the giant's world, Jotunheim, they stopped at a farmhouse to spend the night.

Thor wanted to thank the farmer and his wife for their hospitality by cooking a goat stew for them. He slaughtered and skinned his goats and put them in the pot. Seeing his hosts' shocked looks, Thor said, "Don't worry about the goats. Just make sure you put all the bones, whole, into the skins I've laid out." The family did as he commanded, except for the farmer's son, Thjalfi, who cracked open one of the thigh bones to get at the marrow.

The next morning, Thor took the goatskins full of bones out into the courtyard and blessed them with his hammer, Mjolnir. Instantly, the goats popped back up, full of life once more. The only problem was that one of them was lame in one leg.

"Someone broke a bone, didn't they?" said Thor through gritted teeth. His brows furrowed, he gripped Mjolnir with white knuckles, and storm clouds gathered. Seeing his anger reaching a boiling point, the family became frightened.

"Please, my lord," pleaded the farmer, "take my son, Thjalfi, and my daughter, Roskva, as servants to compensate you for this offense." Thor calmed down and accepted their offer. Thjalfi and Roskva packed their things, and Thor left the goats at the farm to recover.

The foursome departed and soon entered a dark forest. Toward evening they found a place to pass the night, a large building that was completely open on one side. But when they tried to sleep, thunderous roaring and a quaking of the ground kept them awake. They moved farther back in the building, taking refuge in a side chamber, but they still didn't get much sleep.

In the morning, a groggy Thor discovered that there was a giant sleeping—and snoring—not far away, and he realized what had caused all the noise during the night. This wasn't just a giant, it was a GIANT, one who would have towered above the trees if he'd been standing up. At Thor's approach, the giant did just that. For the first time in his life, Thor was unsure if he wanted to start a fight with a giant.

"Ah, good morning, little man," said the giant, yawning. "Hey, I recognize you! You must be Thor of the Aesir, aren't you? My name's Skrymir, by the way. Say, you weren't trying to steal my glove, were you?"

Thor watched as Skrymir picked up the building they'd been sleeping in, and he saw that it was indeed a gigantic glove. The side chamber was just the thumb of the glove! Skrymir settled down for breakfast, and so did Thor and his companions. The giant asked where they were going.

"To Utgard, to test our abilities against the giants there," said Thor.

"Are you now? Big plans for someone so little!" roared Skrymir. "I could accompany you part of the way, if you like. The road could be hazardous for folk such as you."

Thor and Loki conferred, and they agreed that angering the giant wasn't something they should do lightly. They told him he could come along.

"Excellent! And I'll tell you what I'll do: I'll carry all the provisions to save you the trouble," said Skrymir, and he took the knapsack from Thjalfi and put it in a big sack.

Off the giant went, taking long strides that made it hard for the rest of them to keep up. In the evening, they caught up with him under a large oak tree.

"Ah, there you are, little ones," said Skrymir. "I've already eaten, so go have your supper while I get some sleep." He turned over and began snoring immediately.

But when Thor went to untie the giant's sack, no amount of pulling made the knots any looser. Tired, hungry, and faced with another sleepless night, Thor got mad. He whirled Mjolnir and brought it down on Skrymir's head.

"Huh?" said Skrymir as he woke up. "Did a leaf fall on my head? Are you folks done with supper yet? You should really get some sleep."

"We were just about to," said Thor, more afraid than angry at this point.

Around midnight, the snoring that boomed through the forest was again driving Thor mad. He bashed Skrymir right between the eyes with his hammer. But the giant simply sat up.

"Did an acorn just hit me?" asked Skrymir. "What are you doing, Thor?"

Thor replied as he backed away, "I, um, just woke up. But it's only midnight, so I should probably get back to sleep."

Thor went back to bed. Now it wasn't just the snoring, but also the doubts he had about his strength and courage that kept him awake. He decided that if he got the chance to strike again, Skrymir would never wake up. Just before dawn, when he was sure the giant was fast asleep, Thor put on the magic belt that doubled his strength. He charged at Skrymir, leaped into the air, and brought Mjolnir down with both hands against the giant's temple. He felt the hammer sink in up to the handle. Skrymir, however, merely rubbed his temple and yawned.

"There must be birds in this tree above us," said Skrymir. "I think one of them just pooped on my head."

Thor was shocked, but he kept it hidden. They all packed up their things and prepared to head out.

"Here's where I leave you," said Skrymir. "I need to go north, but if you keep going east, you'll arrive at Utgard around noon. A word of advice: Don't try to act tough when you get there. You might think I'm big, but I'm nothing compared to the folks there. And Utgarda-Loki's men won't put up with pipsqueaks like you getting smart-alecky. Or you could turn back now. That's probably a better idea. Ta-ta!"

And with that, Skrymir strode off. Thor and his companions went on, breakfastless, for several hours until they emerged from the forest. There, on an open plain, they saw the biggest castle they'd ever imagined. They had to bend over backward until their heads nearly touched their spines in order to see the top of it. Thor banged at the enormous iron gates but got no answer. When he couldn't wrench the gates open, they all just squeezed into the courtyard through the gap in the bars. Sounds of feasting drifted out of a massive hall, so they went in.

Skrymir hadn't lied. Most of the giants that packed the hall's two gargantuan benches would have stood at least a head above him. Biggest of all was Utgarda-Loki, sitting on his throne at the far end.

"Who is this entering my hall?" asked Utgarda-Loki. "Could that be Thor, the god of thunder? Something must be wrong with my eyes, because I expected someone much bigger." The hall echoed with the giants' laughter.

Utgarda-Loki continued: "If you and your little friends want a seat at our feast, it doesn't come cheap. You need to show us that you have some skill that you're the best at."

"Not a problem!" declared Loki. "I'm the fastest eater there is. I'll challenge anyone, anytime."

"Then let's do it now," said Utgarda-Loki. "My friend, Logi, please come out to challenge this tiny mischief maker."

Logi stepped forward, and he wasn't very tall, so Loki felt he had a very good chance of winning. They brought out a long, wooden platter filled with meats of all kinds and set it in the middle of the floor. Loki and Logi sat at opposite ends, and at the signal to start, they ate their way toward each other. When they met in the middle, however, Loki saw that while he had eaten all the meat, Logi had gobbled up the bones and the platter as well.

"I declare Logi the winner!" shouted Utgarda-Loki.

Then it was Thjalfi's turn. He was a very good runner, so Utgarda-Loki paired him with a wispy-looking man named Hugi. They were to run to the gates and back. At "Go!" Thjalfi took off; Hugi was nowhere to be seen. But when he returned to the hall, Hugi was waiting at the finish line. The same thing happened in the second race. In the third race, Thjalfi had just touched the gate and was turning back when he saw Hugi trotting up to him; he had already crossed the finish line and was coming back to congratulate Thjalfi on his efforts. Utgarda-Loki turned to Thor. "That's two down. Thor, do you have some ability that might impress us? It's not looking too good for the Aesir at the moment."

"Drinking," said Thor. "I can out-drink anybody."

"Very well, but let's test you first to see if you come up to our minimum standards," said Utgarda-Loki. He clapped his hands, and a drinking horn was brought. "The best of us can down this in one gulp. For most, it takes two. But even the wimpiest here can drain the horn dry in three gulps."

Thor looked at the horn. It wasn't that big, but it was long. He hefted the horn and drank. He found that he couldn't lift the point as high as he'd like, but he kept going. When he was completely out of breath, he lowered the horn. He was horrified to find that the level in the horn had hardly gone down at all.

"If you'd told me Thor of the Aesir would need two gulps, I wouldn't have believed you," said Utgarda-Loki.

Thor tried again. He gulped until his face was red and tears were streaming from his eyes, but the liquid was only a finger's breadth lower than before.

"You're toying with us, aren't you, Thor? Saving it all up for one final drink, right?" said Utgarda-Loki.

Thor summoned all his power and anger and drank. He drank until his lungs were about to burst and he was about to pass out. That try made the biggest dent, but the horn was still far from empty.

"All right. That's enough of that," said Utgarda-Loki. "It seems that drinking just isn't your thing. Tell you what. Here's a sport some of the youngsters around here like to do: Pick up my cat. It's not much of a challenge, I'll admit, but you really haven't impressed me that you could handle much more."

A big gray cat slunk into the hall and curled up at the foot of the throne. Thor strode over to it, determined to show that he could do something, *anything*. He put his hands under the cat and lifted. It was heavier than it looked, but just as he was making some headway, the cat arched its back. Thor strained, stretching his arms over his head and standing on his tiptoes, but the best he could do was to lift one paw off the ground.

"Well, that went about as well as I expected," said Utgarda-Loki. "I mean, look at the size of you!" The giants' laughter raised the roof.

"I might be smaller than you," growled Thor, "but now I'm angry, and I want to fight! Pick anybody, and I'll take them on!"

"Hmmm…. Let me see. I don't know if we have anybody here who would lower himself to fight a weakling like you," said Utgarda-Loki. "Oh, I know. Bring in my old nurse, Elli. She'd enjoy wrestling you."

A bent old crone shuffled into the hall, and Thor ashamedly faced off against her. But the harder he pushed, the firmer she stood. He tried, but she tested every muscle in his body, looking for a weak spot. She pushed back. His body ached with the effort of keeping her off of him. Eventually she got him down to one knee.

Utgarda-Loki stood up. "Stop the match! No point in going on, or challenging anyone else here to fight," he said. "I'll tell you what. Since it's now so late, I'll let you and your friends stay the night. I'd feel bad if I sent you away and something terrible happened to you."

So the giants made room on the bench, and Thor and his companions shared in the feast. The food and drink were excellent, but their mood was such that they didn't enjoy them. Especially Thor. The next day, they were given a load of provisions for the road. Utgarda-Loki himself escorted them from the castle. Once outside, he addressed them.

"I hope you've enjoyed your stay in Utgard, but if I have anything to say about it, you'll never come back again. If I'd known how strong you were, I never would have allowed you in."

"What are you talking about? Strong? I've never felt so small and worthless," said Thor.

"That's because I deceived you with illusions," said Utgarda-Loki. "It was I who met you on the road and called myself Skrymir. I secured the provision sack with magical wire so you couldn't untie it. When you hit me with Mjolnir, I moved a mountainous plateau in front of my head. If you look over there in the distance, you can see the three great valleys you hammered into existence. Any one of those blows would've killed me easily.

"The challenges inside the castle were more trickery. Logi was simply fire I put in the form of a man, and he ate up the bones and platter as easily as the meat. When Hugi beat you in the footrace, Thjalfi, it was because he was my thought, and nothing is faster than a thought.

"And Thor, the horn you drank from was connected to the sea. Although you thought you weren't making any progress in draining it, the tides went out all over the world. My cat was no cat; it was Jormungand, the Midgard Serpent that encircles the earth. Everyone was terrified when you raised one of its feet off the ground. Why, you lifted it nearly up to the heavens! And Elli was actually Old Age. Everyone who tangles with Old

Age eventually gets taken down, but you held your ground and only went down on one knee. That was truly a miracle.

"So, be happy with what you achieved. But if you come back, I'll use tricks even dirtier than these to defend myself."

With a shout, Thor swung his hammer at Utgarda-Loki, but the giant was no longer there. And when he turned around, wanting to smash the castle, he found that it, too, was gone. There was only a wide-open space where it seemed the castle had been.

Annoyed and confused, Thor led his companions back home to Asgard. He never forgot his humiliation in Utgard, and he swore he'd do more than just lift the Midgard Serpent if he ever encountered it again.

Bodvar Bjarki and the Champions of King Hrolf Kraki

Long ago in the Uppdales of Norway, there lived a strong young man named Bjorn. Although he was the son of a king, he loved a commoner named Bera. Bjorn's mother had died, and his father had remarried an evil woman, a sorceress from Lapland named Hvit. When Bjorn refused Hvit's advances, she turned him into a bear; he ran away into the forest and became a terror, eating livestock and wildlife alike.

Bera encountered the bear, and from his eyes she knew he must be Bjorn. She followed him back to a cave, where he was able to take on human form for a short time each day. They lived together, but he sensed that he wouldn't survive this way for long. He needed to hunt as a bear to survive, and one day the king's men cornered Bjorn and killed him. At a feast to celebrate the killing, Queen Hvit commanded Bera to eat some of the bear meat. Bera spit it out, but the queen forced her to eat some. Soon after, Bera gave birth to three boys. They were all strong and a bit strange, and all had taken on some animal instincts and characteristics because Bera had eaten some of that meat.

The first was Elk-Frodi, so called because he was a furry elk from the waist down. He grew fast and had quite a temper; as a boy, he killed or maimed several men while playing sports. Elk-Frodi wanted to leave as soon as he could to make his fortune in the world, so his mother showed him where his father had inserted three handles in the stone walls of a cave. He tried pulling them, one after another, but only the last came out—a short sword, but very strong. He decided to become a bandit, killing men for money on the lonesome roads in the mountains.

Bera's next son had the feet of a dog, so he was known as Thorir Hound's Foot. He was nearly as strong as Elk-Frodi, but not so hot-headed. He pulled a battle-axe from the cave wall and traveled to Sweden, where the Gotar made him their king.

Bodvar Bjarki was the youngest son. He grew into a handsome man, and if he had any animal in him, it didn't show. He did, however, want to avenge his father, Bjorn. He walked right up to the king's hall and into the queen's bedroom, and before she could use her sorcery on him, he threw a leather bag over Queen Hvit's head and beat her to death. When the old king died, Bodvar could have ruled the kingdom, but he decided he wanted to be someone's champion instead. His mother, Bera, showed him the last handle in the cave, and he pulled out a powerful sword. But the weapon was unruly and hard to manage, and every time it was drawn it had to kill a man.

Bodvar traveled into the mountains to visit Elk-Frodi. His brother invited him to share the life of a bloodthirsty bandit, but that wasn't in Bodvar's nature. Before he left, Elk-Frodi stamped his hoof into a rock. He said that if the hoofprint filled with earth, then he'd know Bodvar had died from sickness; if it filled with water, he had drowned; but if it was filled with blood, he'd been killed with a weapon, and Elk-Frodi would come to avenge him. Bodvar thanked him and went on his way.

Soon he came to the land of the Gotar. His brother King Thorir Hound's Foot welcomed him and offered him noble titles and lands. But Bodvar didn't want any of that, and after a short stay he set off for Denmark. He had heard that the great King Hrolf was the most generous and most just ruler in the Northlands. It was said that he had a magnificent hall filled with the best and bravest champions, and that's where Bodvar wanted to be.

His journey over land and sea to the island of Sjaelland was long and difficult. Riding up to the king's hall at Hleidargard, he saw that a feast was in progress. The king wasn't there, but many of his men were having a rowdy time. As he went to take a seat, he heard whimpering coming from a corner. Investigating, he found what looked like a large mound of bones. A filthy hand reached out of the mound and placed another bone on top.

"Who's that inside there?" asked Bodvar.

"My name's Hott, kind sir," said a weak voice from inside the mound of bones.

"Why are you in there?"

"This is my shield wall, kind sir. I built it to protect me from the bones the warriors throw at me," explained Hott.

That was more than Bodvar could stand. He grabbed Hott's wrist and yanked him out, sending bones scattering everywhere. "Please don't kill me, kind sir!" begged Hott. "My shield wall wasn't yet finished!"

"You and your pitiful shield wall," Bodvar grumbled as he dragged Hott from the hall. He took the man down to a pond and threw him in. He scrubbed Hott clean and dressed him in a new suit of clothes. Soon they were back inside the hall, where Bodvar made frightened little Hott sit next to him. Several of the king's men gave them nasty looks, but Bodvar paid them no mind. A few whipped small bones at Hott's head, but Bodvar seemed not to notice and kept on eating. Hott was about to slink back to his corner when a particularly big warrior hurled a leg bone at them. Bodvar caught it in midair and threw it back, killing the man.

The king arrived and demanded to know what had happened. Both sides told their stories, and King Hrolf could see that his man had been in the wrong. It was behavior the king had warned them about. Still, he demanded compensation for the dead man.

"Would you be willing to take his place in my personal guard?" asked King Hrolf.

"Only if my friend Hott can join me," answered Bodvar.

"Hmmm.... I don't expect to get much service out of him, but I don't see why he can't share our table," said the king.

So Bodvar staked a high place in the hall for the two of them, and that made some of the veteran warriors resentful. Few would talk to them, and most shot them dirty looks whenever they saw them. Then around the time of the winter solstice, Bodvar noticed that the men seemed very quiet and looked worried. He asked Hott about this.

"It's because of the troll," explained Hott, shivering. "It's come the past two winters to raid the king's cattle. It's a horrible beast—absolutely huge! And it has wings on its back, too. The king has lost many champions to it."

King Hrolf put out the word that he wanted everyone to stay inside at this time of year, no matter what happened to the cattle. Bodvar, of course, didn't listen. He sneaked out one night and forced Hott to come along.

"That thing will be the death of me!" cried Hott.

"Oh, I don't think it'll be as bad as that," said Bodvar. "It might even be an improvement."

Before long they heard a roaring, and the troll bounded out of the forest, held aloft by its great wings. Mouth wide open and claws flashing, it came for them. Hott wailed like a baby, and Bodvar pushed him into the bushes. As the beast charged, Bodvar went to draw his sword—but it wouldn't budge! He tugged with all his might, but it refused to leave its sheath. Finally, with the monster almost upon him, he ripped the scabbard away and drove the sword point into the creature's heart. The troll dropped dead immediately.

"Now, Hott, you'll drink its blood and eat its heart," said Bodvar. Hott refused, but Bodvar was insistent, and eventually Hott drank two big mouthfuls of blood and ate some of the heart. He felt the change immediately, as strength and courage flowed into him. Bodvar tested him by trying to wrestle him to the ground, but Hott stayed on his feet.

"You won't have to be scared of those men anymore," said Bodvar.

"Or be scared of *you!* Ha, ha!" crowed Hott.

Together they propped the monster back up on its feet and went home. In the morning, a guardsman came running to the king, saying that the monster had been spotted on the road, coming this way. King Hrolf and his champions armored up and headed out. They could see the troll in the distance, and even though it wasn't moving, no one seemed eager to get any closer.

"I'll slay it for you, my king," said Hott, "or I'll die trying. I only ask that you lend me your sword, Gullinhjalti, so I can do the job."

"This sword can only be wielded by a brave and skilled fighter," said King Hrolf.

"You have described me perfectly," said Hott. He accepted the sword and walked right up to the monster, knocking it over with one blow.

"Bodvar, am I correct in guessing that he had help in killing the troll?" asked the king in a whisper.

"Maybe," was Bodvar's reply.

"Ha! No matter. I can see the amazing change you brought about in him," said Hrolf. "That's an even bigger feat than slaying the troll."

King Hrolf let Hott keep the sword, and he said that Hott should now be called Hjalti, after the sword. Hjalti got more respect after that, and he was accepted as one of the king's 12 champions. But he never used his newfound strength to punish those who had bullied him. For that they called him Hjalti the Magnanimous.

***

Long before all of this happened, King Hrolf's stepfather, King Adils of Sweden, had asked for Hrolf's help in a battle against King Ali of Norway. Adils had promised vast rewards, and although Hrolf's forces were crucial to his victory, miserly Adils had never paid up. When Bodvar found out about this, he urged Hrolf to collect and right this wrong. Hrolf agreed.

King Hrolf and his champions crossed the sea and rode from Denmark to Uppsala. The townspeople turned out to greet them and see them in their gleaming armor. Adils made a show of welcome, but when they were all inside the royal hall, armed men stepped out from behind the tapestries and attacked them. Hrolf and his men fought back with a fury, killing most of the Swedes and driving the rest out the door.

Adils was angry that he'd been unable to kill his stepson, or even see which of the men was King Hrolf. He tried to calm things down by inviting everyone back inside, saying it had all been a misunderstanding. When the Danish troops sat down, Adils had his men pile kindling higher and higher onto the fire in the middle of the hall. He hoped that Hrolf would reveal himself because he wouldn't be able to stand the heat as well as his champions could. The men's clothes began to burn, but Adils himself seemed to be able to tolerate it because of his knowledge of sorcery.

Bodvar saw what was happening, so he grabbed a servant who was bringing in kindling and threw him onto the fire. Hjalti and the other champions followed suit, using the bodies of the burned men as stepping-stones to cross the fire and charge Adils. But the Swedish king disappeared into one of the pillars and used magic to escape. Once outside, King Adils had his men barricade the doors and close the ventilation holes on the roof. Then they piled brush and kindling against the building and set it on fire. Choking smoke filled the hall, and burning embers drifted down from the rafters.

"I'd rather die by a sword outside than by fire indoors," said Bodvar.

"That sounds like a fine plan," said King Hrolf.

Together they battered the burning wooden walls and broke through into the street. Armored warriors came at them with spears, axes, and swords, though Adils was nowhere to be seen. They fought man to man, hacking through shields and mail coats, pushing toward the stables where their horses were. But when they arrived, they discovered that Adils' men had pulled flesh from their mounts, cut off their tails, and broken their legs. Any hope of escape seemed to be lost.

Just then, Queen Yrsa—Hrolf's mother—arrived with a string of fine horses for them. "You've been given terrible hospitality here in Uppsala, my son," she said. "Please accept these horses as compensation, as well as this." She handed over a large silver horn filled with gold arm-rings. "This is more than you were owed, but I think some interest has built up over time. Also, one of these rings is Adils' most precious heirloom, Sviagris. He'll be devastated to lose it."

Hrolf accepted the treasure-filled horn, thanked his mother, and led his men at a gallop out of town and across the Fyris Plains. They could see Adils and a large troop pursuing them on horseback.

"It seems these men are very excited about catching us," said Hrolf, "and I'm very excited to see them rewarded for their efforts." With that, he tossed gold rings to every side, strewing them over the path behind them as if he were sowing seeds. Adils' men halted, dismounting to scoop up rings.

Adils was furious. He was riding an exceptionally fast stallion, and he shot past his useless men. His spear leveled, he was set to skewer Hrolf. But Hrolf took Sviagris from the horn and threw the ring directly in front of Adils. The Swedish king couldn't resist the chance to recover his dear piece of jewelry. He hung down over one side of the horse and lowered his spear point to collect the ring.

"Ha!" said King Hrolf. "I've made the mightiest of the Swedes stoop like a pig!" He drew his sword, Skofnung, and swung it at Adils as he rode past. The blade sliced his backside clean off, and Adils had to retreat home. Hrolf grabbed Sviagris and rode off with his men.

***

Another strange thing happened while they were returning from this adventure. They came to a farmhouse where a one-eyed old man named Hrani greeted them. He congratulated Hrolf on how well his expedition had gone and offered him a sword, a shield, and a coat of mail. They all looked old, rusted, and in bad repair, and Hrolf politely refused the shabby gifts. The old man was deeply insulted.

"You are not nearly half as wise as you think you are, King Hrolf," said Hrani.

There was no question of their staying the night now, so Hrolf and his men rode off. A short time later, Bodvar called a halt. His face was as pale as a ghost. "I think we've made a grave mistake, my king," said Bodvar. "I think that old man was Odin himself."

"I fear the same thing," said Hrolf.

They rode back to make amends, but the farm and the man were gone.

***

Back in Denmark, they enjoyed a long period of peace and prosperity. But, like all things, this couldn't last forever. King

Hrolf's half-sister, Skuld, was an evil woman steeped in witch-craft from the dark-elvish blood on her mother's side. She was married to Hjorvard, an under-king who owed tribute to Hrolf. She needled her husband endlessly, telling him he could take Hrolf's place if he only had the courage to try. She came up with a plan to visit King Hrolf at Yuletide with their entire entou-rage—which would include every scum, villain, and mercenary they could get their hands on.

When winter came, Skuld and Hjorvard set up their encamp-ment near Hleidargard, King Hrolf's hall. Either they were very good at keeping secrets, or Skuld's sorcery gave the camp an air of innocence, or maybe Hrolf was simply too busy with his own Yule preparations, but no one suspected a thing. That is, until one morning when Hjalti was returning home after a visit to a lady friend. He stumbled into the visitors' camp and saw that it was filled with men in armor, sharpening their weapons and preparing to do battle. He ran back to Hleidargard and reported what he'd seen.

"You'll get no tribute from Skuld and Hjorvard this year or any other, my king! We need to arm ourselves! The enemy is at the gates!" he cried. "Now is the time to repay our king for the gen-erosity he's shown us. You can say I speak from fear if you like, but this may be the last time we fight together, so be ready!"

Bodvar was the first on his feet, followed by all the others. They put on their armor, but as they made for the door, King Hrolf stopped them. "Let us drink and be happy before battle," he said. "Let them know the sort of men they'll be dealing with: the bravest champions ever assembled in the Northlands. Yes, tell Hjorvard and Skuld and all their scoundrels that we will drink and be happy before we collect our tribute."

And so it was. When they finally left the hall, they saw the enemy already drawn up in battle array. Hjalti looked everywhere but didn't see Bodvar. He had little time to wonder about it, however, because the struggle had commenced. Hrolf himself drove ahead with the banners, his champions on each side and the rest of his garrison following. They were outnumbered, but their band stabbed into the heart of Hjorvard's army. Skofnung sliced from side to side, separating heads from necks and limbs from trunks.

Hjalti looked up and saw that a huge bear fought at King Hrolf's side, doing more damage with a sweep of his paw than any five champions could. Blows and missiles bounced off his hide. His teeth crunched any enemy men and horses that came within reach. Panic spread through Hjorvard's ranks. But Bodvar's absence worried Hjalti.

"His place is near the king. Why isn't he here?" asked Hjalti.

"You have to trust him," said King Hrolf. "He is wherever he needs to be. He's proved his valor time and time again."

But Hjalti couldn't accept this, and he raced back to the royal hall. There he saw Bodvar sitting quite still, staring off into space. The sight infuriated Hjalti. "How long are we supposed to wait for our most famous champion?" Hjalti yelled. "Your reputation is in tatters! Get up now and defend your king, Bodvar, or I'll burn down this hall with you in it!"

Bodvar Bjarki summons a bear to battle

Bodvar sighed and stood up. "No use trying to frighten me. I'm ready to go. But I won't be able to give the king as much help out there as I did in here." They went back into the battle, and Hjalti saw that the bear had vanished. He realized then that Bodvar had somehow summoned the bear by means of magic, and breaking his concentration had spoiled the spell.

With the other champions, they fought their way to Hrolf and circled around him. The piles of bodies rose. But once the bear had left, Skuld came to the battlefield and worked her magic. She sent a monstrous boar against them—larger than an ox—and arrows flew from its bristles as it shook itself. Most terrifying of all was seeing mortally wounded men rise back up and rejoin the fray, sporting horrific gashes. Hjorvard himself was one of them, coming back at Bodvar no matter how many times he was dealt a deathblow.

In the end, only King Hrolf, Hjalti, and Bodvar remained. But overwhelmed as much by exhaustion as by their many wounds, finally they, too, fell gloriously. King Hjorvard fell as well, and Queen Skuld was left with only a few troops.

Elk-Frodi was true to his word: When he saw that the hoofprint was filled with blood, he came with the army of Thorir Hound's Foot and soldiers sent by Queen Yrsa. They avenged Bodvar and King Hrolf and made an end to evil Queen Skuld. They raised burial mounds over the king and all his champions, laying their swords by their sides. Finally, they gave Denmark into the hands of Hrolf's daughters before returning home.

Thor and the Clay Giant

When Thor was off fighting trolls in the east, Odin decided to mount Sleipnir and stretch the horse's eight legs. They tore out the main gate of Asgard and thundered across the Bifrost bridge. In almost a blink of an eye they found themselves deep in Jotunheim, the land of the giants. As luck would have it, the place they stopped for a rest was near the home of a particularly huge and evil giant named Hrungnir.

Hrungnir rode out to Odin on a powerful stallion with a golden mane. "That's a good horse you've ridden onto my property," said Hrungnir.

"You won't find a better one, especially not in Jotunheim," said Odin. "I'd bet my life on it."

"Would you, now? Well, I'll take that bet. Yours may be fast, but Gullfaxi here will outdistance him. And then your head will be mine," said Hrungnir, spurring his horse and charging directly at Odin. Odin leaped onto Sleipnir, and the race was on!

They roared through valleys and across rivers. They wove their way among pine trees and galloped over rocky plains. When Odin rode up the rainbow bridge, Hrungnir didn't even notice. He was focused solely on catching Odin and winning the bet. He rushed through the gates of Asgard before he knew it, only stopping when he saw Odin dismounting at the doors of Valhalla.

"Come inside and have a drink. You must be thirsty after that ride," said Odin.

Hrungnir grumbled, but he followed him in. Many of the other gods were there, but only Freyja felt safe enough to approach the enormous giant with a goblet of mead. Hrungnir tossed it aside.

"No! I want the ones Thor drinks out of," growled Hrungnir.

At Odin's urging, Freyja returned with three large drinking horns. Hrungnir gulped down his drinks and demanded more. He soon became very drunk, and his tongue grew bolder. "This is a fine hall you have here. I think I'll take it back to Jotunheim when I leave," said Hrungnir. "And who'll stop me? Huh? None of you weaklings, that's for sure! I'll pound all your heads to dust! All except Freyja and Sif. They're coming with me. But first I'm going to drink all your mead and ale! Ha, ha!"

Odin had enough. The laws of hospitality only went so far. He called on Thor, and in an instant his son burst in with his hammer raised.

"Why is this giant sitting in Valhalla, being waited on by Freyja? This is an outrage!" shouted Thor.

"Odin invited me, so I'm under his protection," answered Hrungnir.

"You'll regret that invitation before you leave," said Thor.

"Oh, so you'd murder a guest? And an unarmed guest at that?" said Hrungnir. "I supposed Thor only pretends to have courage and honor. But if you're a real man, you'll meet me for a duel at Grjotunagard when I have all my weapons."

"So be it," said Thor.

"Bring a second to back you up. You'll need it," said Hrungnir. With that, he mounted and galloped away to Jotunheim.

The giants were understandably concerned when they found out about the duel. Hrungnir was the strongest of them all, and it would be very bad for them if he lost. They decided to build a giant out of clay to be his second at Grjotunagard, at the border between Asgard and Jotunheim. They made the clay giant 27 miles tall and 9 miles across the chest, and they called him Mokkurkalfi. The only heart they could find that was big enough to give him life was a mare's heart.

But Hrungnir was ready. Even unarmed, he was unbelievably tough. His head was stone; his heart was also of stone, and spiky as well. The shield he carried was a massive stone slab, thicker and broader than his whole body. Over his shoulder he carried a stone club bigger than several men. He stood next to the silent clay giant and waited.

Thor approached with his speedy servant Thjalfi, and they watched from the cover of the forest.

"That shield could give my hammer Mjolnir some trouble, even though I'm wearing my belt of divine strength," said Thor.

"Don't worry about that. I'll get him to lower it," said Thjalfi. He ran out of the forest and up to Hrungnir.

"Hey, giant! You're leaving yourself unguarded," warned Thjalfi. "Thor's coming at you from underground! That shield won't do you any good out in front of you!"

Hrungnir quickly dropped his shield and stood on it. He gripped his club with both hands, looking around for any sign of Thor coming up from below. Then he glimpsed flashes of lightning coming from the forest, and soon he heard the roaring thunder of Thor charging at him with Mjolnir swinging. The clay giant's mare heart quaked with fright, and he wet himself.

Hrungnir hurled his stone club with all his giant might. It flew end over end toward Thor as the god of thunder flung his hammer. The weapons met in midair, and the stone club shattered into a million pieces; those pieces became the whetstones used to sharpen blades all over the world. One of the shards smashed into Thor's head and knocked him unconscious, but Mjolnir kept right on flying to its target and caved in Hrungnir's skull. The giant toppled over, and his leg fell across Thor's neck.

Thjalfi attacked the clay giant Mokkurkalfi, hacking away huge chunks with each slash of his sword. The giant quickly tumbled to the ground, leaving Thjalfi a bit disappointed that it had been so easy. He ran to help Thor but couldn't move the giant's leg. The rest of the Aesir arrived and tried to remove it, but no one was strong enough. Then up walked three-year-old Magni, Thor's son by the giantess Jarnsaxa. He threw off Hrungnir's leg and helped his father up.

"I'm sorry I wasn't here earlier, father," said Magni. "I could've knocked that giant into Hel with my bare fist." Thor agreed, and he hugged his son. He gave Hrungnir's horse, Gullfaxi, to Magni as a reward—which made Odin jealous, as he'd wanted the mount for himself as soon as he'd seen it.

***

When Thor was back home in Thrudvangar, they sent for a wise-woman known as Groa to remove the piece of whetstone that was still lodged in his skull. She chanted spells over him, and before long the whetstone loosened and began to come out. That's when Thor looked up and recognized her.

"You're the wife of Aurvandil the Bold," he said.

"Yes, but he's been lost for many months now. I don't know what's become of him," she said, sadly.

"Why, I was with him just the other week!" said Thor. "I met him far to the north in Jotunheim near Niflheim, and I helped him across those icy, poisonous rivers called the Elivagar by carrying him in a basket. Unfortunately, one of his toes was sticking out, and it froze solid. I snapped it off and threw it into the sky, where it became a star. If you look up, you can see it."

Groa looked up, and there it was. The sight filled her with happiness, because it meant her husband would soon be coming home. It made her so happy that she forgot her spell, and the fragment of stone remained stuck in Thor's head.

Now, if you have any whetstones, be sure never to throw them across the room. That makes the one in Thor's head wiggle and causes him great pain. And you definitely don't want to be on Thor's bad side.

The Death of Baldr

"I've been having bad dreams, mother," Baldr the Good said to Frigg. "I approached the Hound of Hel, and he let me pass.

I approached the Gates of Hel, and they opened for me. There was only darkness beyond."

Frigg was silent for a long moment. It was said she knew many things that were going to happen, but she never spoke of them. "Don't be afraid, my son. No one will harm you if I have any power to stop it." She immediately left on a journey and didn't come back for many days.

Not too long after that, Loki returned to Asgard from a trip abroad. At a square in Idavoll, in the middle of Asgard, he found a large throng gathered around Baldr. It was the strangest thing: gods and elves of all sorts were throwing things at him— spears, axes, stones, and even poisonous snakes and flaming torches. But Baldr didn't seem to mind. He was laughing, as a matter of fact, and so was everyone else. Then Loki realized that nothing was hurting him. Not a single thing hurt him the tiniest bit!

Loki was amazed, but even more than that, he was jealous. "Frigg is behind this, for sure. She wouldn't let anything happen to her golden boy," thought Loki, sneering inwardly. He transformed himself into an old woman and paid a visit to Frigg at Fensalir, making a great show of being worried.

"Please, my queen, you must come quickly! A mob is throwing things at your son Baldr!" he cried in an old woman's voice.

"Don't worry for Baldr's safety, my dear. Nothing can harm him. I've collected promises from all things that they won't hurt Baldr," she said.

"All things? Fire and ice? Iron and stone? Wood and poison?" asked Loki.

"All those and many more," said Frigg.

"Everything in all the worlds?"

"Yes, except for this one plant called mistletoe that grows near Valhalla. It seemed too small and young to be of any harm, so I let it be," said Frigg.

The old woman—Loki—thanked Frigg and left. Loki went straight to the mistletoe sprouts and plucked them. He used them to make a dart and then trotted down to where folks were still pelting Baldr with all kinds of things. Standing aside from the crowd was the blind god Hod, another of Odin's many sons.

"Hod," called Loki, "why aren't you throwing things at Baldr like everyone else? I think he would find it an honor if you did so."

Hod answered, "It would be a waste of time. I'd only miss him."

"Not if I guide your hand. Here, hold this stick," said Loki, putting the dart in Hod's grasp. Loki aimed and Hod threw. He was fantastically strong, and the dart struck Baldr right between the eyes. He fell over, dead.

Loki was nowhere to be found.

The Aesir couldn't believe their eyes. They couldn't speak, only weep. The loss of their son devastated Frigg and Odin. When the gods could finally bring themselves to discuss the crime, they called for the one responsible to be executed. But the act had taken place within a holy sanctuary, and the gods were under solemn oaths not to kill each other there. Full of grief, Odin rode into the west and found a giantess named Rind. He fathered a son with her that they called Vali. When Vali was just one night old, before he'd ever washed his hands or combed his hair, he walked right up to Hod and killed him.

The gods laid Baldr in his ship, piled high with wood for a funeral pyre. Mourners came from all over, filing past to pay their respects. Baldr's widow, Nanna, collapsed from grief and died on the spot. They laid her body next to Baldr's. Odin placed his prized arm-ring Draupnir on Baldr's chest and whispered into his ear; just what he whispered is one of the great unanswerable questions of the world.

When it came time to launch the ship, however, it refused to budge. Thor pushed as hard as he could, but nothing could move it. The gods sent for a giantess named Hyrrokkin, known to be skilled in sorcery. She arrived riding a wolf, using adders for reins. With a single touch she sent the ship out to sea, burning brightly.

Through her tears, Frigg spoke to the assembly of gods: "Who among you has the courage to ride to Hel and beg for Baldr to return? You would have my undying love and gratitude if you could bring my boy back!"

"I'll go, gladly," said Hermod the Bold. He borrowed Odin's horse Sleipnir and took off on the road to Hel. For nine nights he rode through dark valleys and barren plains, until he crossed the bridge across the Gjoll River and knew he was close. Up ahead he saw the hound Garm guarding the gates of Hel. Knowing that he wasn't welcome here as one of the living, Hermod urged Sleipnir forward and jumped both the hound and the gate in a single go.

He rode right up to Hel's hall and pushed his way inside. There the Queen of the Dead sat on her black throne. Baldr and Nanna had been given places of honor, but their gloom was unmistakable.

"Great mistress Hel, I've come to plead for Baldr's life. The Aesir have never known such sorrow. I beg you to let me bring him home. The whole world mourns," said Hermod.

Hel smiled cruelly. "Prove to me that the whole world mourns," she said. "If everything, living or dead, sheds tears for Baldr, then I'll let him leave. But if a single being refuses, then here he'll stay until the end of the world."

Hermod was in a hurry to return with this news, but Baldr stopped him to hand him the golden arm-ring Draupnir to give back to Odin. Nanna also gave him gifts: a linen robe for Frigg and a finger-ring for Frigg's handmaiden Fulla. Hermod said farewell and sped back to Asgard.

The gods sent messengers everywhere. In all the heavens and all the worlds, everything cried for Baldr. People, animals, trees, stones, and the very earth itself—all shed tears and wailed in mourning. Only when the messengers entered a certain cave did they find someone who wouldn't do so. She appeared to be a giantess, and she called herself Thakk.

"I never got anything from Odin's son," she said, "so dry tears is all you'll get from me. Let Hel keep what's hers."

Loki could not be found anywhere, but it was agreed that he must have been Thakk.

Later, at a banquet hosted by Aegir, Loki made an appearance. He openly insulted all the gods, accusing them of weakness, stupidity, cowardice, and lewd acts—without any evidence to back it up. He simply didn't care what they thought of him anymore. Only when Thor threatened to beat his brains out did Loki run off.

Odin sat in his all-seeing throne to look for him; he soon found that Loki had taken the form of a salmon and was living in a river. The gods got a net and dragged it through the river. Loki tried to leap over it, but Thor caught him in midair.

They decided that the death that Hod had received was too good for Loki. The Aesir dragged him to a cave and brought his sons before him. They turned one son into a wolf and had it tear the other son to pieces. Then they used his guts to bind Loki to slabs of stone; those bonds turned to iron. They hung a snake over his head, endlessly dripping venom, stinging his eyes and burning his mouth and nose. Loki's wife, Sigyn, held a basin out to catch the poison, but when it was full and she went to empty it, poison fell again on his face. That made him scream and struggle in agony, and his movements caused earthquakes.

And there he was to lie in torment until the end of the world.

Sigyn watches as Loki suffers for the death of Baldr

The Doom of the Gods

Odin had known since the coming of the three norns, the goddesses of fate, that no one could escape his or her destiny—not even the gods. Still, he did everything in his power to find out what was planned for the gods, in order to prepare. He sacrificed an eye for a drink from Mimir's Well, but all that told him was that he had much more to learn. He stole the mead of poetry from the giant Suttung and nearly lost his life in the process. Poetry helped him see things in a different light, but it didn't reveal the future. He decided he needed to sacrifice himself—to himself. He hung for nine nights on Yggdrasil, the world-ash tree, with a spear wound in his side. No one brought him food or drink. His sight grew dim, and he went a little mad. Finally he saw the secrets of the runes drifting before his eyes. He snatched them up even as he fell to the ground, screaming.

With the magical knowledge he now had, he called up the spirit of a wise-woman from the nether realms. She was a seeress, and she spoke in verse of things yet to come—especially Ragnarok, the Doom of the Gods.

"Garm bays loudly before Gnipa cave,

breaks his fetters and freely runs.

The fates I fathom, yet farther I see:

of the mighty gods the engulfing doom."

Understanding her puzzling words took all of Odin's hard-won wisdom, but he was eventually able to piece together her prophesy.

First will come the Fimbulvetr, or Mighty Winter: three years of bitter cold with no summers in between. This will cause famine and bloody wars throughout Midgard, the world of humankind. Chaos will reign as the order of the universe begins to crumble. On the morning of the last day, when the sun rises one final time, Gullinkambi the rooster will crow to awaken the Aesir. Then the two evil wolves, Skoll and Hati, will finally catch the sun and the moon and devour them, plunging the world into darkness.

Only then will Loki snap his bonds and be free to lead a vast army of the dead from Hel. He has thought of nothing but revenge on the gods for punishing him for Baldr's death. Loki will bring with him three of his children: the earth-encircling serpent Jormungand, the hound of Hel called Garm, and the monstrous wolf Fenrir, released from his magical fetters. The frost-giants, led by Hrym, will join them, sailing toward Asgard on a ship made from the fingernails of all the corpses from the beginning of time. From the far south will come the hordes of Muspelheim led by Surt, a fire-giant wielding a sword that burns more brightly than the sun.

Heimdall, guarding the rainbow bridge Bifrost, will marshal the Aesir by blowing his horn—but that won't stop the inevitable. The gods and the chosen heroes of Valhalla will strap on their war gear and ready their weapons. Odin will ride to Mimir's Well one last time to consult with the well-keeper. The giants will thunder over the blazing Bifrost, which will shatter under their weight once they are safely across. The armies will face off on Vigrid, a battlefield measuring a hundred leagues (300 miles) on each side. Their battle cries will echo across all the worlds as the legions charge and clash.

Thor will hammer his way across the battlefield, crushing the skulls of giants and sending their lifeless bodies flying. His one goal will be to reach Jormungand, the Midgard Serpent. With a mighty leap, he'll bring Mjolnir down on the monster's head. But the dying serpent will spray venom over Thor, killing him.

Loki and Heimdall will face off, fated to slay each other. Likewise, Garm and the one-handed god Tyr will tangle, each dying at the other's hand. The god Frey will wish he still had his best sword when he meets Surt; but he won't, and the fire-giant will cut down the pride of the Vanir.

Frigg will know her second great sorrow (after the death of her son Baldr), as the enormous wolf Fenrir runs forward and swallows Odin whole. Then Odin's silent son Vidar will step forward to avenge the All-Father. Wearing a thick shoe made from the cast-off pieces of shoemaking since the world began, he will step on Fenrir's lower jaw and force the upper jaw skyward, tearing his mouth apart. Then Vidar will cut out the wolf's heart.

When the battle has run its bloody course, Surt will throw fire across the world and scorch the earth's surface with his flaming sword. But the seeress had said that this would not be the end, for gods or for humans. Fresh earth will rise from the sea, and crops will grow without being planted. Before the wolf catches her, the sun will have a daughter as beautiful as she, who will travel the path of her mother. And hidden away in the foliage throughout the battle, a woman and a man called Lif and Lifthrasir will survive to repopulate this green new world.

Odin meets Fenrir at Ragnarok

A place in a higher heaven called Gimle will be a refuge for some. Odin's sons Vidar and Vali will live through the battle and the fire and will return to Idavoll, where Asgard once stood. Joining them will be Magni and Modi, the sons of Thor, and they will bring Thor's hammer, Mjolnir. Baldr and his unintentional killer, Hod, will return from the dead, and all will be reconciled. Hoenir will be a new priest for the gods, casting rune sticks to foretell the future.

The gods will find in the grass the golden playing pieces with which they amused themselves when the world was young. Peace and innocence will rule once again—at least for a little while.

GODS, HEROES, AND MONSTERS:
AN ENCYCLOPEDIA OF NORSE MYTHOLOGY

If you've been a bit confused by some of the stories you've read—well, you can't say we didn't warn you. What follows is a guide to the major people, places, and objects in Norse mythology. When you come across a name and can't remember if it's a goddess or a river, just refer to this guide. Besides the names from the stories in this book, some names from other Norse legends have been included, too. Of course, there are dozens more—giants, dwarfs, swords, troll-wives, and others—just waiting for you to discover!

All names are stressed on the first syllable (AE-sir, for example).

Adils: A legendary Swedish king known for being really cheap. He ruled at Uppsala and was the stepfather of Denmark's King Hrolf Kraki. He refused to pay Hrolf and his warriors for their help in defeating a rival king, and when they came to collect, he tried to have them roasted alive! See Bodvar Bjarki and the Champions of King Hrolf Kraki, page 137. Adils had two famous horses: Slongvir, said to be faster than any other horse, and Hrafn, taken from King Ali. Hrafn stumbled as Adils rode him around a temple of Freyja during a sacrifice, throwing the king to the ground and dashing his brains out.

GUIDE TO PRONUNCIATION

A   as in "father"

E   as in "men"

I   as in "ravine"

O   as in "omit"

U   as in "rule"

Y   as "oo" in "book"

AE   as "ai" in "hair"

OE   as "u" in "slur"

EI   as "ay" in "pay"

EY   as "oy" in "boy"

AU   as "ou" in "house"

G   as in "go"

J   as "y" in "yellow"

H   as a normal "h" in English unless it comes before "v," when it sounds more like "k"

Aegir: The god of the sea, and sometimes a name for the sea itself. Aegir lived on the island of Hlesey (now Læsø, Denmark) and was skilled in magic. His wife was Ran, and his daughters were the waves: Bara, Blodughadda, Bylgja, Dufa, Hefring, Himinglaeva, Hronn, Kolga, and Unn. While Aegir wasn't listed among the Aesir, but as one of the giants, he was given a warm welcome when he visited the gods in Asgard. (His wife Ran was one of the Asynjur, the goddesses of the Aesir.) Aegir's conversation with Bragi, the god of poetry, became the basis for the "Skaldskaparmal" section of the *Prose Edda* (see Eddas, page 43). Aegir was also the brewer of ale for the gods. He used glowing gold to illuminate his hall, and that's why gold is sometimes called "Aegir's fire." Gymir and Hler are alternate names for Aegir and the sea (see The Death of Baldr, page 155).

Aesir (singular As): The gods of Asgard. The Aesir were considered younger and separate from the gods of the Vanir of Vanaheim, but sometimes the term was used for gods in general—as when Frey and Freyja, both Vanir, were numbered among them. Their ruler was Odin, called the All-Father, who was literally the father of many of the gods. The Aesir represented order in the universe, opposing the forces of chaos personified by the Jotnar (giants). See The Origin of the Cosmos and the Coming of the Gods, page 76.

Alf: (1) The singular form of Alfar; an elf. (2) The proper name of a certain dwarf. (3) The stepfather of Sigurd Fafnisbani (see Otter's Ransom, Sigurd, and the Cursed Treasure, page 109).

Three goddesses of the Aesir (left to right): Sif, Frigg, and Idunn

Alfar (singular Alf): Elves. These magical beings were split into two races: the fair Ljosalfar (light-elves), who lived in Alfheim and also in the heavens Andlang and Vidblain even higher up; and the ugly Dokkalfar (dark-elves), who made their homes deep underground away from the light of the sun. Using an elf's name in a kenning (a kind of metaphor) was considered a compliment.

Alfheim: The world of the Ljosalfar (light-elves) in the heavens. Alfheim was also the realm of Frey, who received it from the gods as an infant when he cut his first tooth (see Frey's Courtship, page 124).

Alfrodul: "Elf Disk," another name for Sol (Sun).

Ali: (1) Another name for Odin's son, Vali. (2) A legendary king of Norway.

Alsvinn: One of the horses that pulled the chariot of the sun.

Alvis: A dwarf who tried to take Thor's daughter, Thrud, as his wife. By asking Alvis questions, Thor delayed him long enough for the sun to turn him to stone.

Andhrimnir: The cook of Valhalla, whose name meant "Sooty-in-the-Face." Each day Andhrimnir prepared the boar Saehrimnir in the cauldron Eldhrimnir, although it wasn't known for sure what (or if) the warriors of Valhalla actually ate.

Andlang: A heaven higher and to the south of Asgard. Ljosalfar, the light-elves, were the only beings who lived there. The name means "extended."

Andvaranaut: "Andvari's Gift," a magical arm-ring that made gold multiply. When forced to part with it, the dwarf Andvari cursed the ring so that it would bring death and misery to whoever owned it. This was the most valuable item in the treasure hoard captured by Sigurd from the dragon Fafnir (see Otter's Ransom, Sigurd, and the Cursed Treasure, page 109). Buckets of blood were spilled until the ring was lost forever in the Rhine River. An alternate meaning of the ring's name is "Unwanted Gift."

Andvari: A dwarf whose name means "watcher." He lived deep underground in the world of the Dokkalfar (dark-elves). When the gods were forced to pay compensation for the death of Otr (Otter), Loki went down and captured Andvari, who was in the shape of a fish. To be set free, Andvari had to give up all his treasure, including the magic ring Andvaranaut. Andvari cursed the ring to be the death of whoever possessed it (see Otter's Ransom, Sigurd, and the Cursed Treasure, page 109).

Angrboda: A giantess whose name means "boder of ill." With Loki as the father, she gave birth to at least three great evils destined to bring woe to the gods: the monstrous wolf Fenrir, the world-encircling serpent Jormungand, and the goddess Hel, "the lady of the dead." Angrboda was likely also the mother of Garm and many other giants in wolf shape; all wolves are said to be descendants of Angrboda and these wolf-shaped giants. She lived in the monster-infested Ironwood forest east of Midgard (see Loki's Dangerous Children, page 86).

Arvak: One of the horses that pulled the chariot of the sun.

Asgard: The home of the Aesir in the heavens, including the walls surrounding it (see The Origin of the Cosmos and the Coming of the Gods, page 76). The many fabulous places and halls within Asgard include Valhalla, Idavoll, Gladsheim, Vingolf, Valaskjalf, and Vigrid—the field of battle for Ragnarok (see The Doom of the Gods, page 162). The only way to get to Asgard from Midgard, where humans live, is by crossing the rainbow bridge Bifrost, guarded by the god Heimdall. The walls of Asgard were heavily damaged during the ancient war between the Aesir and the Vanir, but a giant builder and his horse Svadilfaeri rebuilt them. Loki's cunning and Thor's might ensured that the work was done for free (see Loki and the Builder, page 82).

Ask: The first man. Created by three Aesir from a log found on the seashore, his name means "Ash." His wife (also created from a log) was Embla, or "Vine," and from this couple the entire human race descended. Icelandic storyteller Snorri Sturluson identified the creator gods as the sons of Bor (Odin, Vili, and Ve), while in the *Poetic Edda* they are called Odin, Hoenir, and Lodur. One of the gods gave breath and life to the humans, the second gave thought and movement, and the third gave them a face, speech, hearing, and sight (see The Origin of the Cosmos and the Coming of the Gods, page 76).

Asynjur (singular Asynja): The goddesses of the Aesir, considered just as holy and as powerful as their male counterparts. The Asynjur were prayed to for protection and to sanctify oaths and partnerships. Snorri Sturluson listed the

Asynjur as: Bil, Eir, Freyja, Frigg, Fulla, Gefjun, Gerd, Gersemi, Gna, Hlin, Hnoss, Idunn, Ilm, Jord, Lofn, Nanna, Njorun, Ran, Rind, Saga, Sif, Sigyn, Sjofn, Skadi, Snotra, Sol, Syn, Thrud, Var, and Vor. Sometimes the valkyrjur (including the norn called Skuld) were counted among the Asynjur.

Atli Budlason: A legendary king and the brother of Brynhild. Historians feel he was a fictionalized version of the actual historical barbarian king Attila the Hun. Atli married Gudrun, Sigurd's widow. He invited her brothers, Gunnar and Hogni, to his stronghold, only to capture and execute them. In revenge, Gudrun murdered Atli's two sons, stabbed Atli in his sleep, and set fire to his hall (see Otter's Ransom, Sigurd, and the Cursed Treasure, page 109).

Atrid: Possibly "Attacker by Horse," another name for Odin.

Audhumla: The first cow. She rose from the mists of Ginnungagap, the gap where the world began. The four rivers of milk that flowed from her udders fed Ymir, the most ancient of frost-giants. As Audhumla licked salty stones, she slowly uncovered a man's body: Buri, the father of Bor and the grandfather of Odin (see The Origin of the Cosmos and the Coming of the Gods, page 76). Her name could be used as a kenning (or metaphor) for "cow" in a poem.

Aurboda: A mountain-giantess, the wife of Gymir and the mother of Gerd (see Frey's Courtship, page 124).

Aurgelmir: The frost-giants' name for Ymir, the oldest member of their race.

Aurvandil: The husband of the sorceress Groa. Thor had carried him safely out of the giant world Jotunheim in a basket, but the cold froze one of Aurvandil's toes. Thor snapped it off and threw it into the heavens, where it became a star. Groa was so happy to hear that her husband would soon be home that she forgot the spell she needed to remove a piece of whetstone from Thor's head (see Thor and the Clay Giant, page 151).

Austri: A dwarf whose name means "easterly." Austri and his brothers Nordri, Sudri, and Vestri held up the sky made from Ymir's skull (see The Origin of the Cosmos and the Coming of the Gods, page 76).

Baldr: One of the Aesir, and the son of Odin and Frigg. Icelandic poet Snorri Sturluson called him "the wisest of the Aesir and most beautifully spoken and the most merciful." Baldr the Good was incredibly handsome, and it's said that light shone from him (see Of Apples and Nuptials, page 102). He made his home at Breidablik with his wife, Nanna. His son was Forseti. When Baldr dreamed of his own death, Frigg traveled all the worlds securing promises from everything to never harm Baldr—but she neglected to get an oath from the mistletoe plant. Jealous Loki made a dart of mistletoe and gave it to the blind god, Hod, to throw at Baldr, and it killed him instantly (see The Death of Baldr, page 155).

Baleyg: "Fiery-Eyed," another name for Odin.

Bara: A daughter of Aegir and Ran, whose name means "wave."

Baugi: A giant and the brother of Suttung, who was the keeper of the magical mead of poetry. Odin, in disguise, labored for

Baugi one summer doing the work of nine men, hoping to be paid with the magical mead. Suttung refused his request, and Baugi attempted to kill Odin when the god tried to steal the mead. Odin escaped, however, and brought the secret of poetry to the gods.

Beli: A giant killed by Frey with an antler.

Bera: The mother of Elk-Frodi, Thorir Hound's Foot, and Bodvar Bjarki (see Bodvar Bjarki and the Champions of King Hrolf Kraki, page 137).

Bergelmir: A wise giant who was a sort of Noah before the world was created. When the gods killed the frost-giant Ymir, his blood drowned the entire race of frost-giants—except for Bergelmir, who escaped by floating off in a large box with his wife (see The Origin of the Cosmos and the Coming of the Gods, page 76).

Berserkir (singular berserkr): Fierce warriors, possibly especially dedicated to Odin. They appear in sagas as members of kings' war-bands or as opponents for heroes to overcome. Snorri Sturluson said that they "went to battle without armor and acted like mad dogs or wolves. They bit into their shields and were as strong as bears or bulls. They killed men, but neither fire nor iron harmed them. This madness is called 'berserkr-fury.'" There's some debate about the meaning of the name. "Berserk" can mean "bare shirt," referring to the fact that they fought without armor. Or it can mean "bear shirt," possibly referring to the bearskins they wore or to their bearlike nature as they charged into battle. When the full "berserkr-fury" was upon them, they were considered half man and half beast.

Bestla: Odin's mother. She was the daughter of the giant Bolthorn and was married to Bor, son of Buri (see The Origin of the Cosmos and the Coming of the Gods, page 76).

Biflindi: Another name for Odin.

Bifrost: The rainbow bridge reaching up to Asgard, guarded by Heimdall at a place called Himinbjorg at the edge of heaven. Bifrost burned with a divine flame, preventing the giants from scaling it to attack the gods. Nevertheless, when Ragnarok comes, Surt and his hordes from fiery Muspelheim will thunder over the bridge, shattering it in the process (see The Doom of the Gods, page 162).

Bil: One of the Asynjur, the goddesses of Asgard. With Hjuki, she is a companion of Mani, accompanying him on his nightly journey guiding the moon across the sky.

Bileyg: "One-Eyed," another name for Odin.

Bilskirnir: Thor's hall, located in his realm of Thrudvangar in Asgard. This was said to be the largest building ever built, containing 540 apartments.

Bjorn: A king's son turned into a bear by the wicked sorceress Hvit. He was the father of Elk-Frodi, Thorir Hound's Foot, and Bodvar Bjarki (see Bodvar Bjarki and the Champions of King Hrolf Kraki, page 137).

Blodughadda: A daughter of Aegir and Ran, the personification of an ocean wave.

Bodvar Bjarki: One of King Hrolf Kraki's 12 champions. There are many similarities between Bodvar and the legendary

Anglo-Saxon hero Beowulf. Bodvar Bjarki was the son of Bera and Bjorn. His father had been transformed into a bear, which gave Bodvar some of his bearish character (Bjarki means "little bear"). Bodvar had two brothers: Elk-Frodi, who was an elk from the waist down, and Thorir Hound's Foot, who had a dog's feet. Bodvar traveled to join King Hrolf's retinue at Hleidargard in Denmark. There he befriended a man named Hott, slew a winged troll that had been attacking the king's hall, and proved himself the equal of the king's berserker. He fought bravely on the expedition to Sweden when King Adils proved to be so treacherous, though he later fell in battle along with King Hrolf and all of his champions (see Bodvar Bjarki and the Champions of King Hrolf Kraki, page 137).

Bolthorn: A giant, the father of Odin's mother Bestla (see The Origin of the Cosmos and the Coming of the Gods, page 76).

Bolverk: "Evildoer," another name for Odin.

Bor: The father of Odin, Vili, and Ve. He was the son of Buri. In some poems, his name is spelled Bur (see The Origin of the Cosmos and the Coming of the Gods, page 76).

Bragi: The god of poetry, renowned for his wisdom, eloquence, command of language, and long beard. He was especially celebrated for his knowledge of poetry. In the poem "Grimnismal" in the *Poetic Edda*, he was reckoned the best of all the skalds (poets). His wife was Idunn, keeper of the apples of youth (see Of Apples and Nuptials, page 102). Bragi's conversation with the god Aegir explaining the doings of the Aesir opens the section of the *Prose Edda* called "Skaldskaparmal" ("The Language of Poetry"). See Eddas, page 43.

Breidablik: The home of the god Baldr in heaven. The name means "broad gleam," and there was no place more beautiful.

Brimir: (1) A hall in heaven filled with drink and good cheer for those who could reach it. (2) A sword carried by Odin.

Brisingamen: Freyja's famous necklace. Its name means "shining necklace," and it was supposedly made by four dwarfs. (By some accounts, Freyja slept with them to get it.) Loki once stole Brisingamen, but the guardian Heimdall went after him; after a battle in which both transformed themselves into seals, Heimdall was the victor. Thor wore the necklace when he disguised himself as Freyja to get his hammer back from the giant Thrym (see Thor the Bride, page 97).

Brokk: One of the dwarf brothers who forged the golden arm-ring Draupnir, the gold-bristled boar Gullinbursti, and the magic hammer Mjolnir. Loki wagered his own head that Brokk and his brother couldn't produce anything to match what the sons of Ivaldi had made—Sif's golden hair, the magical ship Skidbladnir, and the spear Gungnir (see Loki's Head Wager, page 90.)

Brynhild: A valkyrja and the sister of King Atli Budlason. When Sigurd Fafnisbani discovered her magically asleep in a hall surrounded by fire, he leapt the flames and awakened her. They fell in love. But Grimhild wanted Sigurd for her daughter Gudrun; she gave Sigurd a potion that erased his memory of Brynhild. Later Sigurd disguised himself as Gunnar to win her hand for him, but jealousy arose between Brynhild and Gudrun. Brynhild convinced Gunnar and his brothers to kill Sigurd—then, overcome with grief and remorse, she ran herself through with a sword and was burned on Sigurd's funeral pyre (see Otter's Ransom, Sigurd, and the Cursed Treasure, page 109).

Bur: Another spelling of Bor, the father of Odin.

Buri: The very first god, Odin's grandfather. When Audhumla the first cow licked stones, a man's hair was revealed, then his head, and finally his whole body. It was Buri, who was big, powerful, and handsome. His son was Bor (or Bur). See The Origin of the Cosmos and the Coming of the Gods, page 76.

Byleist: One of Loki's brothers.

Bylgja: A daughter of Aegir and Ran; her name means "billow."

Dag: "Day," son of Nott (Night) and the god Delling. He rode behind his mother, circling the earth every 24 hours in a chariot pulled by his horse Skinfaxi (see The Origin of the Cosmos and the Coming of the Gods, page 76).

Dain: One of the stags that lived in the branches of the World-Ash, Yggdrasil, and nibbled on its foliage.

Delling: One of the Aesir. With his wife, Nott, he was the father of Dag (Day).

Disir (singular Dis): Female guardian spirits, such as might be called on to aid in childbirth.

Dokkalfar (singular Dokkalf): Evil-natured "dark elves" with hides blacker than pitch. Also known as Svartalfar ("black-elves"), they lived deep beneath the earth. (Dvergar, Dokkalfar, and Svartalfar might have been different words for the same beings.)

Draupnir: A magical golden arm-ring that dropped eight copies of itself every nine days. Forged by the dwarf brothers Brokk and Eitri to win a bet with Loki, the ring came to be in Odin's possession (see Loki's Head Wager, page 90). After Odin's son Baldr was killed, Odin placed the ring on his funeral pyre and it went with him to Niflheim. When Odin's son Hermod traveled down to plead with Hel to let Baldr return but was refused, he was only allowed to take Draupnir back to Odin (see The Death of Baldr, page 155).

Drofn (also Dufa): A daughter of Aegir and Ran, the personification of an ocean wave.

Duneyr and Durathror: Two stags living in the branches of the world-ash tree, Yggdrasil, and nibbling on its foliage.

Durin: The second of the original dwarfs created from the body of Ymir, the original giant.

Dvalin: (1) One of the stags living in the branches of the world-ash tree, Yggdrasil, and nibbling on the foliage. (2) One of the first dwarfs. "Dvalin's drink" is one way to refer to the mead of poetry.

Dvergar (singular Dverg): Dwarfs. Originally maggots that came from the blood and flesh of the giant Ymir, the dwarfs were granted consciousness by the gods. These pale beings lived deep underground in the realm of the Dokkalfar, and they were skilled in crafting magical treasures that even the gods found priceless. If caught above ground when the sun rose, they could turn to stone. (Dvergar, Dokkalfar, and Svartalfar might have been different words for the same beings.)

Eikthyrnir: A stag that stood atop Valhalla nibbling at the leaves of the tree called Laerad—also known as Yggdrasil, the world-ash. Water dripped from its antlers, flowing into a multitude of rivers that crisscrossed Asgard. Some poured into Midgard, the world of humans; some even spilled down into the pool called Hvergelmir in Niflheim, where icy rivers flowed out beneath the lowest root of Yggdrasil.

Einherjar: "Single Warriors," the name given to those who'd fallen in battle and were deemed worthy to serve Odin in the afterlife and be his adopted sons. They lived in Valhalla (some were said to live in Vingolf or Gimle), and each day they put on their armor and took up their weapons to do battle with one another. At dinnertime, the fallen picked themselves up and joined the victors for a feast, with mead and ale served to them by the valkyrjur. When Ragnarok comes and the giants attack Asgard, the einherjar are to take the field on the side of the gods in a doomed attempt to keep the world from ending.

Eir: One of the goddesses of Asgard, said to be an excellent doctor.

Eitri: One of the dwarf metalsmiths who created the golden arm-ring Draupnir, the gold-bristled boar Gullinbursti, and Thor's hammer, Mjolnir (see Loki's Head Wager, page 90).

Elivagar: "Stormy Rivers," the collective term for the poisonous, icy rivers flowing out of the spring Hvergelmir in Niflheim. Individually, these rivers were Fimbulthul, Fjorm, Gjoll, Gunnthra, Hrid, Leipt, Slid, Svol, Sylg, Vid, and Ylg.

Eljudnir: Hel's great hall that faced north on the Nastrand, the shore of the dead. Its walls were woven of snakes' bodies, their mouths spitting venom; venom also dripped down through ventilation holes in the roof. Wading through these indoor rivers of poison were liars and murderers.

Elk-Frodi: A brother of Bodvar Bjarki, born with the body of an elk from the waist down. Elk-Frodi was the strongest of the three brothers, and before he was 12 years old he had crippled or killed several grown men while sparring. He only had a short sword, given to him by his father, but he found that it could pierce rock. Because he was too violent for human company, he went alone into the mountains to become a bandit. Elk-Frodi promised to avenge Bodvar if he should die by a weapon, and he did just that (see Bodvar Bjarki and the Champions of King Hrolf Kraki, page 137).

Elli: "Old Age," personified as an old crone. Thor was tricked into wrestling her in the stronghold of the giant Utgarda-Loki, but she only managed to get him down onto one knee (see Thor's Journey to Utgard, page 128).

Embla: The first human woman. The gods made her from a log, as they did her husband, Ask (see The Origin of the Cosmos and the Coming of the Gods, page 76).

Fafnir: Originally a giant, Fafnir and his brother Regin killed their father to get the treasure the gods had paid as compensation for killing their brother Otr (Otter). Fafnir took the treasure for himself and transformed into a dragon to defend it, but the hero Sigurd was able to slay him with the sword called Gram (see Otter's Ransom, Sigurd, and the Cursed Treasure, page 109).

Farbauti: A giant, the father of Loki. His wife was Laufey or Nal (see The Origin of the Cosmos and the Coming of the Gods, page 76).

Feng: "Gain," another name for Odin.

Fenrir: A monstrous wolf, one of the evil offspring of Loki and the giantess Angrboda. Also known as Vanargand and Hrodvitnir, he was the father of Skoll and Hati. Seeing how big he was getting, the gods knew they had to chain this monster. After he burst two sets of shackles, they fashioned a special chain called Gleipnir and tricked Fenrir into trying it on (see Loki's Dangerous Children, page 86). The gods chained him to a rock on the Island of Lyngvi, with a sword shoved between his jaws to keep him from biting anyone. The drool from his mouth formed the River Van. Fenrir was destined to thrash about until Ragnarok, when he would break free and devour Odin. Then Vidar would avenge his father's death by ripping the wolf's jaws in half (see The Doom of the Gods, page 162). An alternate name for Fenrir is Fenris Ulf.

Fensalir: The magnificent hall in Asgard where Odin's wife Frigg lived (see The Death of Baldr, page 155).

Fimbulthul: One of the poisonous, icy rivers known as the Elivagar that flowed out of Hvergelmir spring in Niflheim.

Fimbultyr: "Great God," another name for Odin.

Fimbulvetr: "Mighty Winter," three seasons of intense cold with no summer in between, signaling the beginning of Ragnarok (see The Doom of the Gods, page 162).

Fjallar: One of the dwarfs who killed the god Kvasir to make the mead of poetry from his blood. After they also killed the parents of the giant Suttung, he and Gallar took the mead from them as compensation.

Fjolnir: "The Concealer," another name for Odin.

Fjolsvid: (1) Another name for Odin. (2) The giant gatekeeper who met Svipdag at the entrance to Lyr, the hall where the maiden Menglod lived, when the hero was on a quest to win her hand.

Fjorgvin, Fjorgynn: Said to be the father of Odin's wife Frigg (see The Origin of the Cosmos and the Coming of the Gods, page 76).

Fjorgyn: Another name for Jord, Thor's mother.

Fjorm: One of the poisonous, icy rivers known as the Elivagar that flowed out of the spring of Hvergelmir in Niflheim.

Folkvang: "Battlefield," the realm of Freyja, goddess of love, in Asgard. She chose half of those slain each day to live with her there in the hall called Sessrumnir; Odin got the rest.

Forseti: One of the Aesir, the son of Baldr and Nanna. At his gleaming hall, Glitnir, he settled all arguments and legal disputes. Whoever came to him with a quarrel left satisfied that it had been judged fairly (see Of Apples and Nuptials, page 102).

Freki: "Greedy," one of Odin's pet wolves. He fed his wolves from the table at Valhalla, since he had no need for food himself.

Frey: The god of fertility, rain, sunshine, growing things, and wealth. People prayed to Frey for peace and prosperity. Though he was a Van, he was reckoned the most glorious of the Aesir. His father was Njord of Noatun and his sister was Freyja, goddess of love. He was the lord of Alfheim but could be found traveling far and wide, either in his chariot drawn by the enormous boar Gullinbursti or in his fabulous folding ship Skidbladnir (see Loki's Head Wager, page 90). Also known as Yngvi-Frey, he was said to be the ancestor to the royal lines of Sweden and Norway. He gave up his trusty magical sword (which could fight on its own) to marry the beautiful Gerd (see Frey's Courtship, page 124). Because of this, he had to use improvised weapons when he fought the giants Beli and Surt; the first he defeated, but the second killed him at Ragnarok and burned the world to a cinder (see The Doom of the Gods, page 162).

Freyja: The goddess of love, and the most beautiful of either the Vanir or the Asynjur goddesses. Second in rank only to Frigg, she was considered the most approachable of the goddesses; people prayed to her about matters of the heart. Her father was Njord, and Frey was her brother. Her husband Od was frequently away, causing her to shed tears of gold. A pair of cats pulled her chariot as she traveled the worlds looking for Od, using names such as Mardoll, Horn, Gefn, and Syr when she was in exotic foreign lands. Their daughters were Hnoss ("Treasure") and Gersemi ("Jewel"). Freyja often visited battlefields, dividing

freyja, goddess of love

the fallen warriors with Odin and bringing hers to live in the hall of Sessrumnir in Folkvang, her realm in Asgard. Her prized possessions were a cloak of falcon feathers that allowed her to fly and the priceless necklace Brisingamen—but it was Freyja herself that giants most frequently wanted to steal (see Loki and the Builder, page 82, Thor the Bride, page 97, and Thor and the Clay Giant, page 151).

Frigg: The wife of Odin and the queen of the Aesir. She was the daughter of Fjorgvin, and her son was Baldr; she lived in the hall of Fensalir in Asgard (see The Origin of the Cosmos and the Coming of the Gods, page 76). Like Freyja, Frigg had a falcon cape for flying. Her attendants were the goddesses Gna, Fulla, Hlin, and Lofn. It was said that Frigg knew the fates of all men but chose not to give out that information. The first of the two great sorrows in her life was the death of Baldr despite all her efforts to prevent it (see The Death of Baldr, page 155). The death of Odin in the jaws of the wolf Fenrir was the second (see The Doom of the Gods, page 162).

Frost-giants: See Hrimthursar and Jotnar.

Fulla: One of the Asynjur goddesses, she was Frigg's hand-maiden and shared all her secrets. A virgin, she let her hair flow free with only a golden headband to control it. Fulla carried a wooden box containing Frigg's belongings and looked after her shoes (see The Death of Baldr, page 155).

Gallar: One of the dwarfs who killed the god Kvasir to make the mead of poetry from his blood. After the dwarfs also killed the parents of the giant Suttung, he and Fjallar took the mead as compensation.

Gangleri: "Way-Weary," another name for Odin.

Garm: Hel's hound, chained to guard the mouth of Gnipahellir ("Jutting Caves"), the entrance to the dark world of Niflheim (see The Death of Baldr, page 155). Also called Moongarm, he was one of the evil offspring of Loki and Angrboda and fed on the blood of the dead. His howling and breaking free from his chains (like Fenrir) would signal the start of Ragnarok. It was prophesied that he and the god Tyr would kill each other in that final battle (see The Doom of the Gods, page 162).

Gaut: "God of Goths" (possibly meaning "God of Men"), another name for Odin.

Gefjun: A virgin goddess, one of the Asynjur. She called to her all girls who died unmarried. It was said that she'd plowed a trench in Sweden and it had filled with water to become Lake Mälaren; the plowed earth flew up and landed next to Jutland to become Denmark's island of Sjaelland.

Gefn: A name for Freyja, the goddess of love.

Geirrod: A clever giant who once captured Loki and forced him to bring Thor to his hall without his hammer, iron gloves, or girdle of might. On the way, they met with Grid, a friendly giantess who warned Thor and lent him her own gauntlets, girdle of strength, and strong staff. With these Thor was able to cross a swiftly rising river and break the backs of Geirrod's daughters when they tried to crush him against the ceiling. Finally Geirrod threw a lump of molten iron at Thor, taking cover behind an iron pillar. Thor caught the lump and sent it flying back through the pillar, through Geirrod, and through the back of the hall.

Gerd: The wife of Frey and the daughter of Gymir and Aurboda of the mountain-giants. Frey saw her by means of Odin's magical throne, Hlidskjalf, and found her so beautiful that he thought he'd die unless he had her. He begged his servant Skirnir to try to win her over for him, giving him his sword as a reward—something he'd later regret (see Frey's Courtship, page 124).

Geri: "Ravener," one of Odin's wolves that ate the scraps from his table at Valhalla.

Gersemi: A daughter of Freyja and Od. Her name means "Treasure" or "Jewel."

Gimle: Above and to the south of Asgard was another heaven, Andlang, and above that was Vidblain. In this third heaven was Gimle, a hall more beautiful than gold and gleaming more brightly than the sun. The souls of the good and righteous would live there forever and ever, even after Ragnarok (see The Doom of the Gods, page 162).

Ginnungagap: The "Mighty Gap" of nothingness between freezing Niflheim and burning Muspelheim, where the world and life began. The frost-giant Ymir (aka Aurgelmir) emerged from the dripping of melting ice there, and the gods formed the heavens and the earth out of his body (see The Origin of the Cosmos and the Coming of the Gods, page 76).

Gjallarhorn: (1) The "Loud Horn"—the guardian Heimdall's trumpet—used to warn the Aesir of approaching danger. (2) The horn that Mimir uses to drink from his well of wisdom—possibly the same as Heimdall's trumpet.

Gjoll: One of the poisonous, icy rivers known as the Elivagar that flowed out of the spring of Hvergelmir in Niflheim. A golden bridge crossed it on the road to Hel, and the river passed very near the Helgrind, the gates of Hel.

Gjuki: A king who was the father of Gudrun (wife of Sigurd Fafnisbani), Gunnar, and Hogni (see Otter's Ransom, Sigurd, and the Cursed Treasure, page 109).

Gladsheim: The temple of the Aesir, located at the center of Asgard in the place called Idavoll. Built entirely of gold, it contained 13 thrones: one for Odin plus a dozen for the other male gods. Nearby were Vingolf, the temple of the Asynjur, and Odin's hall Valhalla.

Glapsvid: Another name for Odin.

Gleipnir: The chain the gods used to tie up the wolf Fenrir. When two sets of iron fetters failed, Odin sent Frey's messenger Skirnir down to the world of the Svartalfar, the dark-elves, to have a stronger one made. They called it Gleipnir, and the seemingly delicate silken ribbon was constructed from the sound of a cat's footstep, a woman's beard, a mountain's roots, bear's sinews, a fish's breath, and bird spit—in other words, mostly out of nothing at all. Fenrir was tricked into allowing the gods to bind his legs with Gleipnir (see Loki's Dangerous Children, page 86). The chain was fated finally to break on the day of Ragnarok.

Glitnir: The god Forseti's hall in Asgard, where he settled disputes. The walls and columns were made of gold, and it was roofed with silver.

Gna: Frigg's messenger and one of the Asynjur goddesses. She traveled to many worlds, carrying out missions for the queen of the gods. Her horse, named Hofvarpnir, could gallop across sea and sky.

Gnipahellir: The "Jutting Caves" that formed the entrance to Hel's realm, guarded by her watchdog Garm.

Gnita Heath: Where Fafnir the dragon (formerly a giant) had his lair and hid his treasure (see Otter's Ransom, Sigurd, and the Cursed Treasure, page 109).

Gondlir: "Bearer of the Magic Wand," another name for Odin.

Gram: Sigurd Fafnisbani's sword. Regin forged it from the shards of Sigurd's father's sword. Gram was so sharp that when it was stuck into a river it cut in two a tuft of wool that floated against the blade, and it was so strong that Sigurd hacked an anvil in half with it. With Gram in hand, Sigurd avenged his father, Sigmund, and slew Fafnir the dragon (see Otter's Ransom, Sigurd, and the Cursed Treasure, page 109).

Grani: Sigurd Fafnisbani's horse. Gray in color and descended from Odin's horse Sleipnir, Grani was chosen by Sigurd on the advice of Odin (in disguise, of course). He was Sigurd's loyal companion for the rest of his life, carrying the treasure hoard from Fafnir's lair and leaping the wall of fire to awaken Brynhild. Grani mourned Sigurd when he died (see Otter's Ransom, Sigurd, and the Cursed Treasure, page 109).

Grid: A giantess, the mother of Vidar with Odin.

Grimnir (shortened form Grim): The "Cowled One," another name for Odin.

Grjotunagard: The place on the border with Jotunheim, the giants' world, where Thor killed the giant Hrungnir (see Thor and the Clay Giant, page 151).

Groa: (1) A sorceress who tried to remove a fragment of whetstone from Thor's head after his battle with the giant Hrungnir. Overjoyed when told that her husband, Aurvandil, would soon be home, she forgot her spells and the whetstone stayed put (see Thor and the Clay Giant, page 151). (2) Also a sorceress (possibly the same one), she's summoned from the grave by her son Svipdag to give him magical aid in his quest to win the maiden Menglod.

Gudrun: Sigurd Fafnisbani's wife, the daughter of King Gjuki and Grimhild, and the sister of Gunnar, Hogni, and Guttorm. Her jealous dispute with Brynhild led to the death of both Sigurd and their son, Sigmund. Gudrun's mother then married her off to King Atli. When Atli attacked Gunnar and Hogni for Sigurd's treasure, Gudrun fought alongside her brothers. In the end, Atli had Gunnar and Hogni executed. In her grief, Gudrun killed her own sons by Atli, ran a sword through Atli, and burned his royal hall to the ground (see Otter's Ransom, Sigurd, and the Cursed Treasure, page 109).

Gullfaxi: "Gold Mane," the horse of the giant Hrungnir. After Thor killed the giant, he gave Gullfaxi to his young son Magni to thank him for lifting the dead giant's leg off him. Odin wasn't pleased—he'd wanted the horse for himself (see Thor and the Clay Giant, page 151).

Gullinbursti: "Golden Bristles," the boar of the god Frey that was forged by the dwarf brothers Eitri and Brokk (see Loki's

Head Wager, page 90). Also known as Slidrugtanni, the boar sometimes pulled Frey's chariot and sometimes bore him on its back. It could run across sea and sky faster than any horse, and the light it shed from its bristles trumped any darkness—even that of the underworld. Not surprisingly, the boar was an animal considered sacred to Frey and was used in sacrifices to him.

Gullinhjalti: "Golden Hilt," the sword given by King Hrolf Kraki to Hjalti the Magnanimous (formerly known as Hott).

Gullinkambi: "Golden Comb," the rooster who is to crow over the Aesir on the morning of Ragnarok (see The Doom of the Gods, page 162).

Gulltopp: "Gold Forelock," the horse of Heimdall, guardian of the gods.

Gullveig: A witch or goddess, possibly one of the Vanir. It was said she could cast spells on the mind. The Aesir tried to kill her three times by burning her, but each time she was reborn. Nevertheless, their attempt led to the world's first war, fought between the Aesir and the Vanir (see Loki and the Builder, page 82).

Gungnir: The spear of Odin. The dwarf brothers known as Ivaldi's sons created the spear at Loki's request so he could get back in the All-Father's good graces after he'd cut off Sif's hair. It was said that nothing could stop Gungnir's thrust (see Loki's Head Wager, page 90).

Gunnar Gjukason: Son of King Gjuki and brother of Gudrun, Hogni, and Guttorm. When he wanted to marry Brynhild but neither his horse nor Sigurd's would carry him over the flames surrounding her hall, Sigurd offered to do it for him, disguised as Gunnar. When Brynhild found out about the deception she goaded her brothers to kill Sigurd. Later, their sister's new husband, King Atli, attacked Gunnar and Hogni after they refused to give up Sigurd's treasure. Atli threw Gunnar into a snake pit to die, but he was able to play a harp so skillfully that the serpents fell asleep—except for one, which killed him (see Otter's Ransom, Sigurd, and the Cursed Treasure, page 109).

Gunnlod: A giantess, the daughter of Suttung and the keeper of his mead of poetry. Odin seduced her and she allowed him three drinks of the mead; he instead drank all that was in the three vats before escaping.

Gunnthra: One of the poisonous, icy rivers known as the Elivagar that flowed out of the spring of Hvergelmir in Niflheim.

Guttorm Gjukason: The brother of Gunnar, Hogni, and Gudrun and the son of King Gjuki. He murdered Sigurd Fafnisbani while the hero was sleeping, but Sigurd lived long enough to hurl his sword at Guttorm and slice him in two (see Otter's Ransom, Sigurd, and the Cursed Treasure, page 109).

Gymir: (1) The father of Gerd, the god Frey's wife (see Frey's Courtship, page 124). (2) An alternate name for both Aegir, god of the sea, and the sea itself, meaning "Engulfer."

Haenir: Another spelling of Hoenir, one of the Aesir gods.

Har: "One-Eyed" or "High One," another name for Odin.

Harbard: "Graybeard," another name for Odin.

Hati: The wolf that pursued the moon and was doomed to swallow it at Ragnarok (see The Doom of the Gods, page 162). He was the son of the monstrous wolf Fenrir (aka Hrodvitnir). See The Origin of the Cosmos and the Coming of the Gods, page 76.

Hefring: One of Aegir's daughters, the personification of a wave.

Heidrun: A goat that stood atop Valhalla, nibbling at the leaves of the tree called Laerad—also known as Yggdrasil, the world-ash. The goat's udders gave mead instead of milk, enough to fill up an enormous vat each day from which all the einherjar—the fallen warriors serving Odin—could drink until satisfied.

Heimdall: Guardian of the gods. He lived at Himinbjorg near the bridge Bifrost and was constantly on watch so he could warn the Aesir if giants invaded. Heimdall needed less sleep than a bird and could see for more than 300 miles, day or night. He could hear even the sound of grass and wool growing. If danger threatened, the blast of his Gjallarhorn could be heard in all the worlds. Sometimes called a son of Odin, he was also said to have been born to nine virgin sisters (possibly Aegir's daughters). According to one poem, he was the father of the three classes of human beings: thralls (slaves), the freeborn, and nobles. Known as the White God, he was also sometimes called Hallinskidi, Vindhler, Rig, or Gullintanni ("Golden Teeth," since his teeth were gold). See The Origin of the Cosmos and the Coming of the Gods, page 76. Having once tangled with Loki when the trickster god stole Freyja's necklace, he and Loki were fated to kill each other at Ragnarok (see Thor the

Bride, page 97, Of Apples and Nuptials, page 102, and The Doom of the Gods, page 162).

Hel: (1) Goddess of the underworld, the daughter of Loki and the giantess Angrboda. When Odin found out what misery she would cause, he threw her into cold, dark Niflheim. There, in her hall called Eljudnir, she was in charge of the dead of nine worlds who had passed away from sickness or old age, as well as those who'd been wicked in life. Half of her face was black as pitch, the other half pale as a corpse, and she always looked miserable and stern (see Loki's Dangerous Children, page 86). Hel jealously guarded the souls she captured, refusing to release Baldr unless all beings mourned him (which she knew wouldn't happen) (see The Death of Baldr, page 155). It was said that she would send spirits of the dead to aid the forces of chaos when Ragnarok came (see The Doom of the Gods, page 162). (2) The realm of the dead, including Niflhel/Niflheim, the world of darkness.

Helblindi: (1) Another name for Odin. (2) One of Loki's brothers.

Helgrind: The gates of Hel.

Herjan: "Warrior," another name for Odin.

Hermod: Odin's son and messenger. Called "the Bold," he volunteered to plead with Hel for the return of Baldr (see The Death of Baldr, page 155).

Herteit: "Glad in Battle," another name for Odin.

Hildolf: A son of Odin.

Himinbjorg: Where the guardian Heimdall lived at the edge of heaven, near the bridge of Bifrost (see Of Apples and Nuptials, page 102).

Himinglaeva: One of the daughters of Aegir, the personification of an ocean wave.

Himinhrjot: An ox owned by the giant Hymir. Thor used its head as bait when he went fishing for the Midgard Serpent, Jormungand.

Hjalmberi: "Helmet-Bearer," another name for Odin.

Hjalprek: A legendary king of Denmark and the father of Alf, Sigurd's stepfather (see Otter's Ransom, Sigurd, and the Cursed Treasure, page 109).

Hjalti the Magnanimous: Originally called Hott, he was a bit of wimp, used to being abused by King Hrolf's followers, before Bodvar Bjarki arrived. Bodvar defended him, cleaned him up, and boosted his confidence by taking him on a monster hunt. The king was so impressed that he gave him a sword, Gullinhjalti, and named Hjalti after it. Hjalti forgave those who'd been cruel to him, so King Hrolf also called him "the Magnanimous." He served faithfully as one of the king's champions for the rest of his life, though it was he who broke Bodvar's bear-trance during their final battle, unwittingly dooming them (see Bodvar Bjarki and the Champions of King Hrolf Kraki, page 137).

Hjordis: The mother of Sigurd Fafnisbani. Her husband, Sigmund, was killed while she was pregnant with Sigurd. Later, Alf married her. She had saved the shards of Sigmund's sword, Gram, and gave them to Sigurd when he was preparing to kill the dragon Fafnir (see Otter's Ransom, Sigurd, and the Cursed Treasure, page 109).

Hjorvard: A king under Hrolf Kraki, married to Hrolf's half-sister Skuld. At Skuld's goading, he revolted against Hrolf. His forces won the day after a fierce battle, thanks to Skuld's magic, but Hjorvard fell in the fighting (see Bodvar Bjarki and the Champions of King Hrolf Kraki, page 137).

Hlodyn: Another name for Jord, Thor's mother.

Hjuki: The male companion of the goddess Bil. Together they traveled with Mani as he guided the moon across the night sky.

Hler: An alternate name for both Aegir and the sea, meaning "Roarer."

Hlidskjalf: Odin's throne in his silver-roofed hall, Valaskjalf. From there he could see into all worlds and understand everything he saw. When Frey once sat there, he saw and fell in love with Gerd (see Frey's Courtship, page 124).

Hlin: (1) One of the Asynjur. She was a guardian goddess who protected those whom Odin's wife Frigg chose to save from danger. (2) Another name for Frigg.

Hlora: Thor's foster mother.

Hnikar, Hnikud: "Thruster" or "Spear-Thruster," another name for Odin.

Hnoss: Freyja's daughter, whose name means "Treasure."

Hod: The blind god, a son of Odin. Loki guided his arm to throw the mistletoe dart that killed Odin's son Baldr. This was the unluckiest deed ever among gods or men. Vali, the son of Odin and Rind, killed Hod in revenge when he was one night old. Hod would later return from Hel with Baldr when the earth was reborn after Ragnarok (see The Death of Baldr, page 155, and The Doom of the Gods, page 162).

Hoddmimir's Wood: Probably the foliage of Yggdrasil, the world-ash tree, this was said to be the refuge of the last human beings during Ragnarok.

Hoenir: One of the Aesir, given in an exchange of hostages to the Vanir to guarantee the truce at the end of their war. According to the "Prophecy of the Seeress" in the *Poetic Edda*, it was Hoenir (not Odin's brother Ve) who gave senses to the first humans. A good runner, he was sometimes called "Long Foot" or "Mud King." He was accompanying Odin and Loki when Otr (Otter) was killed and compensation had to be paid, setting in motion generations of tragedy (see Otter's Ransom, Sigurd, and the Cursed Treasure," page 109). After Ragnarok, Hoenir was to become a sort of priest for the surviving Aesir and would be able to prophesy the future for the new world (see The Origin of the Cosmos and the Coming of the Gods, page 76, and Of Apples and Nuptials, page 102).

Hofvarpnir: The goddess Gna's horse, which could carry her over the sea or through the skies.

Hogni Gjukason: Brother of Gudrun (wife of Sigurd), Gunnar (husband of Brynhild), and Guttorm, and the son of King Gjuki. He and Gunnar gave in to Brynhild's jealous rage and plotted the death of Sigurd. Later, Gudrun's second husband, King Atli, captured Hogni and Gunnar to get the treasure Sigurd had obtained from the dragon Fafnir. Though Hogni's heart was cut out, he didn't reveal the location of the gold (see Otter's Ransom, Sigurd, and the Cursed Treasure," page 109).

Horn: Another name for Freyja, goddess of love.

Hott: The original name of Hjalti the Magnanimous before he became a champion of King Hrolf of Denmark (see Bodvar Bjarki and the Champions of King Hrolf Kraki, page 137).

Hrafn: "Raven," a horse King Adils of Sweden took from King Ali of Norway. Adils was riding Hrafn around a temple of Freyja during a festival when the horse stumbled, throwing Adils to the ground and bashing his brains out against a rock.

Hraesvelg: A giant in eagle's form who sat at the northern end of heaven. When he took off, the beating of his wings created the winds that swirled all around the world.

Hrani: Another name for Odin (see Bodvar Bjarki and the Champions of King Hrolf Kraki, page 137).

Hreidmar: A giant who was the father of Otr (Otter), Regin, and Fafnir. When Otr was killed by Odin, Loki, and Hoenir (Loki, really), Hreidmar demanded compensation in gold. Loki got the gold from a rich dwarf named Andvari, but the dwarf cursed the treasure. The surviving brothers, Regin and Fafnir, killed Hreidmar when he refused to share the treasure (see Otter's Ransom, Sigurd, and the Cursed Treasure, page 109).

Hrid: One of the poisonous, icy rivers known as the Elivagar that flowed out of the spring of Hvergelmir in Niflheim.

Hrimfaxi: "Frost Mane," the horse that drew the chariot of Nott (Night). The foam that dripped from his bit became the morning dew.

Hrimthursar: Literally "Frost Ogres," referring to frost-giants.

Hringhorni: Baldr's immense ship, where he was laid on his funeral pyre. The ship refused to move when the time came to set the pyre ablaze, so the gods sent for a giantess named Hyrrokkin, who was able to launch it with a single touch.

Hrodvitnir: Another name for Fenrir, meaning "Famous Wolf."

Hrolf Kraki: A legendary king of Denmark. (Kraki means "Climbing Pole," because he was tall and slim.) A figure somewhat like King Arthur, he was especially renowned for the champions (berserkir) with which he surrounded himself, including Bodvar Bjarki and Hjalti the Magnanimous. He quarreled with his stingy stepfather, King Adils of Sweden, over payment for his champions' services; that led to a nearly disastrous expedition to Uppsala, where they were all almost cooked alive. Hrolf finally met his end in battle against his half-sister, Skuld, and her husband, King Hjorvard (see Bodvar Bjarki and the Champions of King Hrolf Kraki, page 137). Bodvar's brothers avenged him by killing Skuld, then setting up Hrolf's daughters to rule over Denmark.

Hronn: "Wave," one of Aegir's daughters.

Hropt: Another name for Odin.

Hroptatyr: "God of Gods," another name for Odin.

Hrotti: A sword that Sigurd got from the treasure hoard of Fafnir the dragon (see Otter's Ransom, Sigurd, and the Cursed Treasure, page 109).

Hrungnir: The strongest of the giants, with a head and heart of stone. He once chased Odin right up to the gates of Asgard, Hrungnir on his horse Gullfaxi and Odin on Sleipnir. When the giant threatened to carry off Freyja and Thor's wife Sif, Thor would have killed him, but shedding blood wasn't allowed in Asgard. Instead they made plans to duel, and the giants constructed an enormous clay figure to aid Hrungnir. But Thor hurled his hammer Mjolnir, breaking Hrungnir's whetstone club and shattering Hrungnir's skull—and that's how whetstones came into the world. The clay giant was hacked into pieces (see Thor and the Clay Giant, page 151).

Hrym: Leader of the frost-giants during the battle of Ragnarok (see The Doom of the Gods, page 162). Icelandic storyteller Snorri Sturluson identified him as the captain of the horrid ship Naglfari (elsewhere, though, he said Loki was to have that role).

Hugi: "Thought," made into the form of a man by the giant Utgarda-Loki to race against Thor's servant Thjalfi. It turned out that no one could outrun thought (see Thor's Journey to Utgard, page 128).

Hugin: "Thought," one of Odin's ravens. At dawn Odin sent his ravens out to fly over the wide world; at dinnertime they'd return and tell him all they had seen.

Hvedrung: Another name for Loki.

Hvergelmir: A spring in the middle of dark Niflheim, under the lowest root of the world-ash Yggdrasil. The serpent Nidhogg lived there, tormenting the bodies of the dead, with countless more snakes all around him. Many rivers—icy, swift, and deep—flowed from this spring.

Hvit: A wicked sorceress from Lapland who turned Bjorn into a bear after he spurned her advances (see Bodvar Bjarki and the Champions of King Hrolf Kraki, page 137).

Hymir: A giant who once went fishing with Thor to capture the Midgard Serpent, Jormungand. Thor used the head of Hymir's ox Himinhrjot as bait, and when he hooked the beast, he drove his feet all the way through the hull of the boat and down to the sea floor as he strained to pull it up. As the monstrous head emerged and Thor prepared to smash it with his hammer, Hymir got scared and cut the line. Thor knocked the giant overboard in anger.

Hyrrokkin: A giant sorceress or troll-wife summoned by the gods to help launch the ship containing Baldr's funeral pyre. She arrived riding a wolf and using vipers as reins, as witches were said to do. The ship had refused to budge, but with a mere touch she pushed it out to sea (see The Death of Baldr, page 155).

Idavoll: The "Shining Plain" in the middle of Asgard, where the temple Gladsheim and the halls Vingolf and Valhalla stood (see The Origin of the Cosmos and the Coming of the Gods, page 76). It was said that the surviving gods would return to live here after Surt's fire burned away the rest of creation at the end of the world (see The Doom of the Gods, page 162).

Idunn: One of the Asynjur goddesses and the wife of the god Bragi. She was keeper of the box containing the magical apples of eternal youth, which the gods ate when they felt old age coming on. With Loki's help, the giant Thjatsi captured her and her apples; under threat of torture, Loki helped get her back (see Of Apples and Nuptials, page 102).

Ifing: The river that marked the boundary between the land of the gods and that of the giants. It was always ice free.

Ilm: One of the Asynjur goddesses.

Jafnhar: "Just as High," another name for Odin.

Jalk: Another name for Odin.

Jarnsaxa: A troll-wife or giantess, and the mother of Magni by Thor (see Thor and the Clay Giant, page 151).

Jarnvidjur (singular Jarnvidja): "Ironwood Dwellers," the troll-wives who lived in that far-off forest and gave birth to giants in wolf form—the ancestors of all wolves.

Jord: "Earth," the mother of Thor, and one of the Asynjur. She was the daughter of Nott (Night), and her father was someone named Annar or Onar. Some sources say that Odin was both her father and her husband (before he married Frigg). Other names for Jord were Fjorgyn and Hlodyn (see The Origin of the Cosmos and the Coming of the Gods, page 76).

Jormungand: The Midgard Serpent, one of the monstrous offspring of Loki and the giantess Angrboda. Odin took one look at it when it was young and threw it into the deep ocean surrounding Midgard. There it grew until it could encircle all lands and bite its own tail (see Loki's Dangerous Children, page 86, and Thor's Journey to Utgard, page 128). The serpent was Thor's greatest enemy, destined to kill him with its last spit of poison at Ragnarok (see The Doom of the Gods, page 162).

Jotnar (singular Jotun): The giants. Like the titans of Greek mythology, they came before the gods and opposed them. Originating from the venomous, icy flow of the Elivagar rivers in the dark world of Niflheim, they were naturally frightful and fierce. They inhabited all sorts of environments, from frosty plains to rocky mountain peaks, to the land of fire. Some were so cunning, wise, and skilled in magic that they could challenge the Aesir on an equal footing, while others were simple brutes interested only in carrying off a goddess or two (almost always including Freyja). Thor, as the defender of Midgard (where humans lived), was the god most frequently off on adventures slaying these monsters. A few giants, however, were on good relations with the Aesir gods and even became the mothers and fathers of their children.

The frost-giants, led by Hrym, and the fire-giants, led by Surt, were fated to march with the forces of evil and chaos against the Aesir at the final battle of Ragnarok.

Jotunheim: "Giant World," the realm of the Jotnar. The giants had several strongholds there, including Thrymheim, Lyr, and Utgard. Sometimes said to be east of Asgard and sometimes north, Jotunheim was where the second root of the world-ash tree Yggdrasil extended, near Mimir's Well (see The Origin of the Cosmos and the Coming of the Gods, page 76).

Kjalar: Another name for Odin.

Kolga: One of Aegir's daughters, the personification of an ocean wave.

Kvasir: Said to be the wisest of the gods. In one story, he was one of the hostages the Vanir sent to the Aesir to end their early war. In another account, he originated from the truce itself: The Aesir and the Vanir had promised peace by spitting into the same vat, and Kvasir emerged from that. Whatever the case may be, Kvasir wandered far and wide spreading his knowledge. A pair of dwarfs named Fjallar and Gallar, however, killed him and mixed his blood with honey. In this way they created the mead of poetry; whoever drank it would become a poet or scholar. Odin, of course, made sure he got his hands on it for the use of the gods.

Laerad: Another name for Yggdrasil, the world-ash tree whose branches grew over Valhalla.

Laufey: Loki's mother by the giant Farbauti. Another name for her was Nal.

Leipt: One of the poisonous, icy rivers known as the Elivagar that flowed out of the spring of Hvergelmir in Niflheim.

Lif: "Life," the last woman of the age. She would survive Ragnarok with her husband, Lifthrasir, to start mankind over again (see The Doom of the Gods, page 162).

Lifthrasir: "Longing for Life," the man prophesied to survive the fire at Ragnarok by hiding in Hoddmimir's Wood (probably the foliage of Yggdrasil). He and his wife, Lif, would live off the dew and breed a new human race (see The Doom of the Gods, page 162).

Ljosalfar (singular Ljosalf): "Light-Elves," magical beings that lived in the heavens among the gods in places such as Alfheim, Andlang, and Vidblain. Ljosalfar were said to be "fairer than the sun to look at." They were particularly associated with the Vanir gods.

Lodur: According to the *Poetic Edda*, the first human beings were brought to life by Lodur along with Odin and Hoenir. (The storyteller Snorri Sturluson, however, gave the credit to Odin, Vili, and Ve.) Lodur was said to have given humans "heat" and a "goodly hue."

Lofn: One of the Asynjur. Couples would pray to this helpful goddess if they had a love that was forbidden; she would get permission from Odin or Frigg to let the union happen.

Logi: "Flame," the personification of fire. The giant Utgarda-Loki pitted Logi against the god Loki in an eating contest. While Loki only ate the meat, Logi consumed the bones and wooden plates as well (see Thor's Journey to Utgard, page 128).

Loki: The trickster god, son of the giant Farbauti and Laufey (or Nal). His brothers were Byleist and Helblindi. By the giantess Angrboda, Loki was the father of Jormungand (the Midgard Serpent), the wolf Fenrir, and Hel (the goddess of the under-world). By his wife, Sigyn, he was the father of Nari (or Narfi) and Vali. Loki was also known by the names Lopt and Hvedrung. In the form of a mare, Loki mated with the stallion Svadilfaeri and gave birth to Odin's horse Sleipnir (see Loki and the Builder, page 82). He took on other shapes as needed—fly, seal, salmon, and giantess, for instance.

By all accounts Loki was very handsome, but he was also spiteful and loved to play nasty tricks on people. For example, he stole Freyja's necklace and cut off Sif's hair (see Loki's Head Wager, page 90). On the other hand, because of him the gods gained some of their most prized possessions: Odin's spear Gungnir, the magical ship Skidbladnir, the gold arm-ring Draupnir, the gold-bristled boar Gullinbursti, and Thor's hammer Mjolnir. But causing the death of Baldr at the hand of Hod—his most evil deed—overshadowed any good he'd ever done. As punishment, Loki was chained up and had to endure snake venom dripping on his face until the end of time (see The Death of Baldr, page 155). He would finally break free at Ragnarok, bringing all the forces of Hel with him to the battlefield of Vigrid. He would then do battle one last time with Heimdall, guardian of the gods, and they would kill each other (see The Doom of the Gods, page 162). As a major god, Loki appears in many myths (see also Thor the Bride, page 97, Of Apples and Nuptials, page 102, Otter's Ransom, Sigurd, and the Cursed Treasure, page 109, and Thor's Journey to Utgard, page 128).

Lopt: Another name for Loki.

Lyr: The hall in Jotunheim, ringed by fire, where the maiden Menglod lived.

Magni: "The Strong," son of Thor and Jarnsaxa. When Thor killed Hrungnir and was trapped under the dead giant's leg, none of the Aesir could lift the leg off—except for three-year-old

Magni (see Thor and the Clay Giant, page 151). It was said that Magni would return to Idavoll in Asgard after Ragnarok with his brother Modi, bringing the hammer Mjolnir (see The Doom of the Gods, page 162).

Mani: "Moon," son of Mundilfaeri and brother of Sol (Sun). The gods gave him the task of guiding the moon, controlling its waxing and waning so that humans could keep track of time. Accompanying him were the goddess Bil and her companion Hjuki (see The Origin of the Cosmos and the Coming of the Gods, page 76).

Mardoll: Another name for Freyja, goddess of love.

Meili: Thor's brother and a son of Odin.

Menglod: A maiden who lived in a fire-ringed hall in Jotunheim, the giants' world. The hero Svipdag was tasked with finding and marrying her.

Midgard: The "Middle Enclosure," the world where human beings lived. The gods surrounded the land with the eyelashes of the original giant Ymir to protect it from the Jotnar, the giants. (This eyelash fortification was called Midgard, too.) See The Origin of the Cosmos and the Coming of the Gods, page 76.

Midgard Serpent: See Jormungand.

Mimir (also Mim): A wise but mysterious being, possibly Odin's maternal uncle. He was the keeper of the well bearing his name, and he charged Odin an eye to drink from it to gain wisdom. The eye remained in the well, from which Mimir drank each day. Mimir was also one of the hostages (along with Hoenir) given by the Aesir to the Vanir gods at the end of their early war. The Vanir thought they'd been given unworthy hostages (after all, they'd sent Njord, Frey, Freyja, and perhaps Kvasir), so they beheaded Mimir. But Odin preserved the head with herbs and chanted spells over it so that Mimir could tell him secrets of far-off places and events (see The Origin of the Cosmos and the Coming of the Gods, page 76).

Mimir's Well: The well of wisdom containing Odin's eye, which he gave to Mimir in return for a drink of its waters. The well sits under that root of Yggdrasil, the world-ash tree, which extends into the land of the frost-giants (see The Doom of the Gods, page 162).

Mjolnir: Thor's hammer. The dwarfs Eitri and Brokk forged it as part of a bet with Loki over who could make the most precious thing; Mjolnir was what put them over the top. Although the handle came out rather short, this hammer would never miss, no matter how hard it was thrown, and it would always return to Thor's hand. The gods all agreed it would provide the best defense against giants (see Loki's Head Wager, page 90). The name "Mjolnir" possibly meant "crusher," from *molva* ("to crush or pound"), or it might have been related to the Russian word *molnya*, meaning "lightning."

Modgud: A maiden who guarded the bridge over the River Gjoll on the road to Hel.

Modi: "The Brave," one of Thor's sons. It was said that he would survive Ragnarok along with his brother Magni.

Modsognir: The first of the Dvergar (dwarfs).

Mokkurkalfi: An enormous clay figure created and brought to life to aid the giant Hrungnir when he fought Thor. He was 27 miles tall and 9 miles across the chest, and the only heart the giants could find that was big enough for him was a mare's heart. Thor's servant Thjalfi destroyed him with little trouble (see Thor and the Clay Giant, page 151).

Mundilfaeri: The father of Mani and Sol. The gods were so angered that he'd named his son and daughter after the moon and sun that they took his children away and stuck them in the sky to guide their namesakes (see The Origin of the Cosmos and the Coming of the Gods, page 76).

Munin: "Memory," one of Odin's two ravens, who spent each day flying over the world so they could report back to him at night on all they'd seen.

Muspelheim: The "World of Fire." Before there was a world, the intense heat of Muspelheim in the south melted the frosts of cold Niflheim in the north and created life in the gap between them, Ginnungagap. The gods took the sparks shooting out from fiery Muspelheim and placed them in the sky as the stars and the sun (see The Origin of the Cosmos and the Coming of the Gods, page 76). At the final battle of Ragnarok, it was foretold, the fire-giant King Surt will lead the Sons of Muspelheim (almost certainly other fire-giants) over the bridge of Bifrost to storm the gates of Asgard (see The Doom of the Gods, page 162).

Naglfari: (1) An enormous ship constructed from the finger-nails and toenails of the dead. It was forecast that it would slip its moorings and set sail at Ragnarok, transporting the forces of chaos to the battle. Historian and storyteller Snorri Sturluson wasn't clear about which these would be: the Sons of Muspelheim, the frost-giants, or Hel's hordes of the dead—or perhaps all of them. Nor was it clear whether Hrym or Loki would captain Naglfari. However, Snorri did advise that the nails of the dead should be clipped before burial or cremation, to delay completion of this dreadful ship. (2) One of the husbands of Nott (Night).

Nagrind: "Gates of the Dead" at the entrance to Hel, the realm of the dead.

Nal: Another name for Laufey, the mother of Loki.

Nanna: The wife of Odin's son Baldr, and one of the Asynjur goddesses. She was the daughter of Nep and the mother of Forseti. At Baldr's funeral she collapsed and died of grief, and she was burned with him. When Odin's messenger Hermod went to Hel to plead for Baldr's release, Nanna sent back with him a linen robe for Odin's wife Frigg and a finger ring-for her handmaiden Fulla (see The Death of Baldr, page 155).

Nari (also Narfi): One of Loki's sons. As punishment to Loki for causing the death of Baldr, the gods transformed Loki's son Vali into a wolf and had him tear Nari to pieces. Then they used Nari's guts to tie Loki to rocks where a snake would drip venom on him until the end of time.

Nastrand: The "Shore of the Dead," where Hel's hall, Eljudnir, stood far from the warmth of the sun.

Nep: The father of Nanna, who was the wife of Odin's son Baldr.

Nidafjoll: "Dark Mountains," a location in Niflheim near where a serpent or dragon called Nidhogg lived.

Nidavellir: "Dark Fields," a place in the north where the dwarfs had a golden hall.

Nidhogg: "Hateful Striker," a monstrous serpent or dragon that lived at the venomous spring of Hvergelmir near Nidafjoll in Niflheim. There he ravaged the bodies of the dead and gnawed on the lowest root of Yggdrasil, the world-ash tree.

Niflheim (also Niflhel): "World of Darkness." This was the gloomy, cold afterlife realm ruled by Hel, reserved for those of the nine worlds who were wicked in life or had died of old age or disease. The hound Garm guarded the entrance to Niflheim, which contained such grim locations as the pool of venom called Hvergelmir and the shore of the dead known as Nastrand (see The Origin of the Cosmos and the Coming of the Gods, page 76).

Njord: One of the Vanir gods who lived among the Aesir, he was the father of Frey and Freyja (by his own unnamed sister). See Frey's Courtship, page 124. He lived at Noatun and ruled over wind, waves, and fire—it was wise to be on his good side when going fishing or embarking on sea voyages. Also known for his wealth, he was the god to pray to if you wanted to get rich. Njord was one of the hostages the Vanir sent to the Aesir as a pledge of truce. He was married to the giantess Skadi, but as she preferred the mountains and he the sea, they alternated homes every nine days, and neither was happy (see Of Apples and Nuptials, page 102).

Njorun: One of the Asynjur goddesses.

Noatun: "Harbor," the place in heaven where Njord had his high-timbered hall.

Nordri: "Northerly," one of the four dwarfs who held up Ymir's skull to be the sky (see The Origin of the Cosmos and the Coming of the Gods, page 76).

Norn: Any one of the goddesses of fate—Urd, Verdandi, and Skuld—who spun out the future for both gods and humans. They were kin to the giants, and it was said that the golden age of the gods ended when they arrived from Jotunheim. There were also minor, personalized norns—both good and evil— who showed up when babies were born in order to determine the course of their lives. This type could come from several races: gods, elves, or dwarfs (see The Origin of the Cosmos and the Coming of the Gods, page 76, and The Doom of the Gods, page 162).

Nott: "Night," mother of Dag ("Day") and husband of Delling, one of the Aesir. She was also the mother of Jord ("Earth") by Annar (or possibly Odin). At one time she was also married to Naglfari (not the ship with the same name). She rode around the world every 24 hours in a chariot pulled by her horse Hrimfaxi (see The Origin of the Cosmos and the Coming of the Gods, page 76).

Od: The husband of Freyja, goddess of love, and the father of Hnoss and Gersemi. His frequent absences on long journeys made Freyja cry tears of gold.

Odin: King of the Aesir, the All-Father. Odin was the god of wisdom, magic, and war. He was the husband of Frigg and the father of Baldr, Thor (by Jord), Vali (by Rind), Vidar (by Grid), and many, many others (see The Origin of the Cosmos and the Coming of the Gods, page 76). He might be found in his halls—Valhalla and Valaskjalf—but was just as likely to be wandering the worlds, either alone or with Loki and Hoenir (see Of Apples and Nuptials, page 102, Otter's Ransom, Sigurd, and the Cursed Treasure, page 109, and Thor and the Clay Giant, page 151). With his valkyrjur, he chose the bravest and mightiest warriors that were slain in battle to serve him in the afterlife. Because of this, he was often blamed for letting the weaker combatants win.

A wily character, Odin often seemed to be motivated by greed—not just for gold, although he did value the arm-rings Draupnir and Andvaranaut—but especially a greed for knowledge. He knew he was fated to die at Ragnarok in the jaws of the wolf Fenrir, so he wanted to know everything: any event that might lead to it, or any sign that it was coming (see Loki's Dangerous Children, page 86, and The Doom of the Gods, page 162). Odin's two ravens, Hugin and Munin, reported to him on happenings around the world each day, and his throne, Hlidskjalf, enabled him to see anywhere in the universe. But in three cases he went to extremes in his quest to know everything: nearly being killed by giants to steal the mead of poetry from the giant Suttung, giving up an eye for a drink of wisdom from Mimir's Well, and sacrificing himself by hanging on Yggdrasil for nine days to learn the secrets of rune magic.

Odin was known by many titles, and he often used false names when he traveled in order to keep his identity a secret (see Bodvar Bjarki and the Champions of King Hrolf Kraki, page 137). He was called Val-Father ("Father of the Slain"), Sig-Father ("Father of Victory"), Herja-Father ("Father of Armies"), Hanga-God ("God of the Hanged"), Hapta-God ("God of Prisoners"), and Farma-God ("God of Cargoes"). Among his aliases were Gagnrath, Harbard, Grimnir, Har, Bolverk, Gaut, and Ygg. As the leader of the Aesir, Odin is featured in almost every myth (see also Loki and the Builder, page 82, Loki's Head Wager, page 90, Thor the Bride, page 97, Frey's Courtship, page 124, and The Death of Baldr, page 155).

Odroerir: The mead of poetry, or perhaps the name of the pot in which it was kept.

Ofnir: "The Entangler," another name for Odin.

Omi, Oski: Other names for Odin.

Otr: "Otter," the son of Hreidmar and the brother of Regin and Fafnir. His killing by Loki and the subsequent compensation in gold demanded by his father set in motion a sad and bloody chain of events for Sigurd and his family (see Otter's Ransom, Sigurd, and the Cursed Treasure, page 109).

Ragnarok: "The Doom of the Gods" (see page 162)—or as storyteller Snorri Sturluson called it, "The Twilight of the Gods"—as revealed in a prophecy telling of the end of the world. First the frigid winters of Fimbulvetr will bring famine and wars to Midgard. The wolves Skoll and Hati will finally catch and devour the sun and the moon. Loki will shatter his bonds and lead an army of giants and the dead to Asgard. From the burning south will come the hordes of Muspelheim, led by Surt. The enormous wolf Fenrir will swallow Odin, only to be ripped apart by Vidar. Thor will slay his nemesis Jormungand but drop dead from the monster's venom. Loki and Heimdall are fated to slay each other, as are Tyr and Garm. Surt will kill the god Frey and scorch the earth with his flaming sword.

But this is not to be the end. Odin's sons Vidar and Vali and Thor's sons Magni and Modi will survive, and Baldr and Hod will return from the dead. And hidden away throughout the battle, a woman and a man named Lif and Lifthrasir will survive to carry on and repopulate a green new world.

Ran: The wife of Aegir, god of the sea, and one of the Asynjur goddesses. It was said that she had a net to catch all who went to sea (see Otter's Ransom, Sigurd, and the Cursed Treasure, page 109).

Ratatosk: A squirrel that lived on Yggdrasil, the world-ash tree. It ran up and down the trunk, delivering insults between the serpent Nidhogg and the eagle that sat in the upper branches.

Regin: The son of Hreidmar and the brother of Otr (Otter) and Fafnir. After Fafnir took the cursed treasure of Andvari and became a dragon, Regin went to be a metalsmith in the court of King Hjalprek. He became foster father to Sigurd, forging the sword Gram and coaching the boy on how to slay the dragon Fafnir. After the deed was done, Regin showed some remorse; Sigurd, fearing he couldn't trust Regin (and on the advice of some birds), cut off his foster father's head and took the treasure for himself (see Otter's Ransom, Sigurd, and the Cursed Treasure, page 109).

Rind: Vali's mother. Probably originally a giantess, she was still counted as one of the Asynjur goddesses. It was said that Odin won her through the use of spells. He fathered Vali with Rind, an outsider at the time, to avenge Baldr's murder by Hod. Vali killed Hod when he was only one night old (see The Death of Baldr, page 155).

Roskva: The sister of Thjalfi. The siblings became servants to Thor after her brother disobeyed the command not to break any bones of the goats the god had prepared for dinner (see Thor's Journey to Utgard, page 128).

Saehrimnir: A boar that was boiled anew each day to feed the inhabitants of Valhalla.

Saga: One of the Asynjur goddesses, she lived at Sokkvabekk in Asgard.

Sad: "Truthful," another name for Odin.

Salgofnir: A rooster that woke the einherjar—Odin's fallen warriors—each morning for combat.

Sanngetal: "Truthfinder," another name for Odin.

Sessrumnir: Freyja's large and beautiful hall in Folkvang, her realm in Asgard. Half of those killed in battle lived out their afterlives with her there (see Thor the Bride, page 97).

Sidgrani, Sidskegg: "Long-Beard," another name for Odin.

Sidhott: "Long-Hood," another name for Odin.

Sif: Thor's wife and the mother of Ull (not by Thor). Loki cut off her beautiful hair as a cruel joke, and the gods forced him to fix his mess. He not only had some dwarfs make her magical golden hair that would fasten to her scalp, but he also got them to create many other valuable treasures for the gods (see Loki's Head Wager, page 90).

Sigmund: The father of Sigurd Fafnisbani. He was killed before Sigurd was born, but his shattered sword—once it was reforged—helped his son slay Fafnir the dragon (see Otter's Ransom, Sigurd, and the Cursed Treasure, page 109).

Sigtyr: "God of Victory," another name for Odin.

Sigurd Fafnisbani: The son of Sigmund and Hjordis, born after his father had been killed. His mother married Alf, and Sigurd grew up in the court of Alf's father, King Hjalprek. Regin was assigned to be his foster father, and he wasted no time in preparing the boy to slay the dragon Fafnir—actually Regin's brother, sitting on a cursed hoard of gold. Sigurd dug a trench in the dragon's path, and when the serpent slithered over him, he killed him with his sword. Advised by birds not to trust Regin, Sigurd chopped off his head and took the treasure for himself. That was how Sigurd got the name Fafnisbani ("Fafnir's Bane").

On his travels, Sigurd freed a valkyrja named Brynhild from a magical sleep; later, he helped his brother-in-law, Gunnar, win Brynhild as his wife by pretending to be him. That became a source of jealousy between Brynhild and Sigurd's wife, Gudrun. Brynhild convinced her brothers that Sigurd must die, and one of them stabbed Sigurd in his sleep (see Otter's Ransom, Sigurd, and the Cursed Treasure, page 109).

Sigyn: The wife of Loki and the mother of Nari (or Narfi), she was one of the Asynjur goddesses. When Loki was bound, she held a basin over his face to catch the drops of poison from the snake above him (see The Death of Baldr, page 155).

Sjofn: One of the Asynjur goddesses, she was especially concerned with pushing men and women toward thoughts of love.

Skadi: The daughter of the giant Thjatsi and the wife of Njord, she was known as the skiing goddess. When the Aesir killed her father, she demanded compensation. They let her choose a husband from among the gods, but only by looking at their feet. Picking the handsomest pair, she was disappointed to find out they belonged to Njord—not Baldr, as she'd hoped. As she was more at home in mountainous Thrymheim and he near the sea, they split their time between the two—but that meant that one was always miserable (see Of Apples and Nuptials, page 102).

Skidbladnir: A magical ship made by a pair of dwarf brothers for Loki, who gave it to Frey. It was big enough to carry all the Aesir at once, and when the sail was hoisted it would take off with a fresh breeze in whatever direction was desired. When not needed, *Skidbladnir* could be folded up like a piece of cloth and kept in a pocket (see Loki's Head Wager, page 90).

Skilfing: Another name for Odin.

Skinfaxi: "Shining Mane," the horse of Dag (Day). Light shone down from his mane as he crossed the sky.

Skirnir: Frey's servant and messenger. He was sent by Odin down to get the dwarfs to make Gleipnir, the chain used to bind the wolf Fenrir (see Loki's Dangerous Children, page 86). And when Frey was lovesick over Gerd, he sent Skirnir to woo her. Knowing the journey and the task would be difficult, Skirnir asked for Frey's sword as a reward, and Frey agreed. Skirnir used every trick in his bag to win the giant's daughter for his master (see Frey's Courtship, page 124).

Skjalf: Another name for Freyja, goddess of love.

Skjold: A son of Odin, said to be the founder of the legendary Skjoldung line of kings in Denmark.

Skofnung: The sword of King Hrolf Kraki. It was called "the best of all swords borne by man in the Northlands," and Hrolf used it to slash the buttocks off King Adils of Sweden (see Bodvar Bjarki and the Champions of King Hrolf Kraki, page 137). It was said that wounds inflicted by Skofnung wouldn't heal unless rubbed with a special stone. To keep its magic at full strength, one shouldn't draw it in front of a woman or let sunlight shine on its hilt. In some stories ("Kormak's Saga" and "Laxdaela Saga"), it was claimed that Skofnung was recovered from Hrolf's burial mound and used by Icelandic men over a couple of generations; Gellir Thorkelsson was the last of these, and supposedly had it with him when he died in Denmark. Skofnung perhaps ended up buried with him in Roskilde Cathedral on the island of Sjaelland.

Skoll: The wolf that chased Sol (Sun) and was fated to catch her at the end of time (see The Origin of the Cosmos and the Coming of the Gods, page 76 and The Doom of the Gods, page 162).

Odin mounted on Sleipnir

Skrymir: The false name that the giant Utgarda-Loki used when he encountered Thor and his companions in the woods (see Thor's Journey to Utgard, page 128).

Skuld: (1) "Future" or "Debt," the name of one of the three main norns (goddesses of fate). (2) King Hrolf Kraki's half-sister, the wife of King Hjorvard. She was a powerful sorceress who could raise her slain warriors from the dead (see Bodvar Bjarki and the Champions of King Hrolf Kraki, page 137). (3) The name of one of the valkyrjur.

Sleipnir: Odin's eight-legged horse, the best and fastest horse in any world. When Loki transformed into a mare to distract the giant's stallion, Svadilfaeri, he became pregnant and later gave birth to Sleipnir (see Loki and the Builder, page 82).

Slid: One of the poisonous, icy rivers known as the Elivagar that flowed out of Hvergelmir in Niflheim. It was filled with swords and knives, and liars, murderers, and adulterers had to wade through its waist-deep waters in the afterlife.

Slidrugtanni: Another name for Frey's golden boar, Gullinbursti.

Slongvir: One of the horses of King Adils of Sweden.

Snotra: One of the Asynjur goddesses, noted for being wise and courteous.

Sokkvabekk: The place in Asgard where the goddess Saga lived. Cool waters flowed all around it.

Sol: "Sun." The gods stuck her in the sky to guide the chariot of the sun to punish her father for naming her after that heavenly body. Sol's horses, Arvak and Alsvinn, were protected from the heat of the actual sun by bellows placed under their shoulders. Skoll the wolf would pursue Sol endlessly across the sky until Ragnarok, when he'd finally catch her. It was said that Sol would have a daughter who would follow her same path when the earth was reborn. Sol was also known as Alfrodul (see The Origin of the Cosmos and the Coming of the Gods, page 76).

Sudri: "Southerly," one of the four dwarfs that held up the skull of the giant Ymir to form the sky (see The Origin of the Cosmos and the Coming of the Gods, page 76).

Surt: A fire-giant and the king of Muspelheim. At Ragnarok he will lead his hordes against the gods, killing Frey and burning the world to a cinder with his flaming sword (see The Doom of the Gods, page 162).

Suttung: A giant who took the mead of poetry away from the dwarfs Fjalar and Gallar as compensation for the deaths of his parents. Odin later stole the mead from Suttung by seducing his daughter (see The Doom of the Gods, page 162).

Svadilfaeri: A stallion owned by a giant builder, instrumental in repairing the walls of Asgard after the Aesir-Vanir war. The builder had asked for the sun and moon and the hand of Freyja if he finished the work in a single winter. When it looked like he was actually going to finish on time, Loki became a mare to distract the stallion—and the work was delayed long enough for the deadline to pass. Some time later, Loki gave birth to the eight-legged horse Sleipnir (see Loki and the Builder, page 82).

Svafnir: "He Who Lulls to Sleep," another name for Odin.

Svartalfar (singular Svartalf): "Black-elves," another name for the evil Dokkalfar who lived deep beneath the earth. (Dvergar, Dokkalfar, and Svartalfar might all have been words for the same beings.)

Sviagris: "The Pig of the Swedes," a gold arm-ring that was a family heirloom of King Adils of Sweden. King Hrolf Kraki took it when Adils tried to have him and his champions burned alive. As they escaped on horseback, Hrolf tossed out some of the treasure they'd stolen, including Sviagris. When Adils bent down to recover it, Hrolf said, "Now I have made the mightiest of the Swedes stoop like a swine!" and hacked off Adils' behind. Hrolf grabbed Sviagris, while Adils sought medical attention (see Bodvar Bjarki and the Champions of King Hrolf Kraki, page 137).

Svidrir (also Svidur): "Wise," another name for Odin.

Svipal: "Changeable," another name for Odin.

Svipdag: (1) A human hero sent on a quest by his evil stepmother to win the hand of the maiden Menglod. To accomplish this, he summoned the spirit of his dead mother, a seeress. She cast spells to protect him. When he arrived at Menglod's hall, he used a false name and got into a question-and-answer session with the watchman (who may have been Odin). In the end, he learned that only Svipdag could enter the hall; in other words, he just had to be himself. (2) One of the champions of Denmark's King Hrolf Kraki.

Svol and Sylg: Two of the poisonous, icy rivers known as the Elivagar that flowed out of the spring of Hvergelmir in Niflheim.

Syn: "Denial," one of the Asynjur goddesses. She was said to guard the doors of halls against intruders, and was called on by defendants in legal cases.

Syr: Another name for Freyja, goddess of love.

Tanngnjost and Tanngrisnir: "Tooth Gnasher" and "Tooth Grinder," a pair of goats that pulled Thor's chariot. They could be slaughtered and eaten but then made whole again in the morning, as long as none of their bones had been broken.

Thakk: "Thanks," the name Loki took when he assumed the form of a giantess. Hel had agreed that Baldr could return from the dead if everything in the world wept for him. This "giantess" refused, so Baldr had to stay with Hel. The gods saw through Loki's trickery and made him pay for it (see The Death of Baldr, page 155).

Thekk: "Welcome One," another name for Odin.

Thjalfi: Thor's servant, considered the fastest of runners. When Thor and Loki stayed at Thjalfi's father's farm, Thor fed everyone by slaughtering the goats that pulled his chariot; he warned them not to break any bones. Thjalfi couldn't help himself and broke one to get at the marrow. The next day, Thor brought the goats back to life but noticed that one had a broken leg. To repay the damage, Thjalfi and his sister Roskva became Thor's servants. Loyal Thjalfi accompanied Thor on several adventures, racing against Hugi ("Thought") and slaying the clay giant Mokkurkalfi (see Thor's Journey to Utgard, page 128, and Thor and the Clay Giant, page 151).

Thjatsi: A giant, the father of Skadi. Thjatsi once captured Loki and made him agree to lure the goddess Idunn outside of Asgard with her apples of everlasting youth. Loki did so, and Thjatsi in the form of an eagle flew away with Idunn. The gods grew old without the apples, and they soon found out that Loki was the culprit. On threat of torture, he borrowed Freyja's falcon cloak and flew off to rescue Idunn. Loki turned her into a nut and flew away with her. Thjatsi pursued, and as he passed low over Asgard, the gods lit a huge pile of kindling and burned off his feathers. He crashed to the ground and was killed by the Aesir (see Of Apples and Nuptials, page 102).

Thor: "Thunder," the son of Odin and the goddess Jord. Vingnir and Hlora were his foster parents. He was the husband of Sif, the father of Modi, Magni, and Thrud, and the stepfather of Ull. Thjalfi and Roskva were his servants. Thor's realm in heaven was called Thrudvangar, and Bilskirnir was his enormous hall. He was also called Asa-Thor ("Thor of the Aesir") and Vingnir (see The Origin of the Cosmos and the Coming of the Gods, page 76).

Called the strongest of the gods (although Magni demonstrated that he was stronger), Thor was the defender of Midgard and Asgard, keeping them free of giants and other monsters. Aiding him in his single-minded pursuit of this task were three magical objects: a belt that doubled his divine strength, a pair of iron gauntlets, and his hammer Mjolnir, which never missed (see Loki's Head Wager, page 90). He traveled the worlds using a chariot drawn by two goats, and for this reason he was sometimes known as Oku-Thor ("Driving-Thor"). He often went off on adventures in Jotunheim, the land of the giants, and his

Thor battles Jormungand, the Midgard Serpent

strength and courage usually made him return victorious (see Thor's Journey to Utgard, page 128). At Ragnarok, however, he was fated to kill and be killed by the serpent Jormungand (see The Doom of the Gods, page 162). As a major god, Thor is included in many myths (see also Loki and the Builder, page 82, Loki's Dangerous Children, page 86, Thor the Bride, page 97, Of Apples and Nuptials, page 102, Thor and the Clay Giant, page 151, and The Death of Baldr, page 155).

Thorir Hound's Foot: The son of Bera and the brother of Bodvar Bjarki. Born with dog feet but otherwise handsome, Thorir became king of the Gotar in Sweden. He helped avenge his brother's death by killing the sorceress Skuld (see Bodvar Bjarki and the Champions of King Hrolf Kraki, page 137).

Thridi: "Third," another name for Odin.

Thrivaldi: A nine-headed giant killed by Thor.

Thror: Possibly "Inciter of Strife," another name for Odin.

Thrud: "Strength," the daughter of Thor and Sif. Her name was listed among both the Asynjur goddesses and the valkyrjur shield-maidens. The dwarf Alvis once tried to take her below ground to be his wife, but Thor delayed him with questions until the sun rose and turned him to stone.

Thrudheim: "The Land of Strength," another name for Thor's realm of Thrudvangar.

Thrudvangar: "Fields of Strength," Thor's realm in Asgard where he had his massive hall, Bilskirnir. It was also known as Thrudheim (see Thor and the Clay Giant, page 151).

Thrungva: Another name for Freyja, goddess of love.

Thrym: "Noisy," a giant king who stole Thor's hammer Mjolnir. He offered to give it back if the gods would hand over Freyja to be his bride. Thor went in her place, wearing her clothes (with Loki dressed as his maid). When the hammer was brought out, Thor grabbed it and unleashed his fury on all the giants present, especially Thrym (see Thor the Bride, page 97).

Thrymheim: A mountainous region in Jotunheim, the giants' world. This was the realm of King Thrym and also the home of Thjatsi and his daughter Skadi (see Thor the Bride, page 97 and Of Apples and Nuptials, page 102).

Thud, Thund: Other names for Odin.

Troll: A general term for "monster." Trolls weren't just humanoid—they came in all shapes and sizes, including boars and dragons—but they were all evil.

Troll-Wife: A giantess or ogress skilled in the magical arts, usually described as riding a wolf and using vipers for reins.

Tyr: The god of war (see The Origin of the Cosmos and the Coming of the Gods, page 76). He was the only one of the Aesir brave enough to stick his hand in Fenrir's mouth when the wolf was being bound, even though he knew it would likely be bitten off (see Loki's Dangerous Children, page 86). Like Odin, he favored battle over arbitration when conflicts arose. He and Garm, the hound of Hel, would make an end of each other at Ragnarok (see The Doom of the Gods, page 162). As a major god, Tyr is often included in myths (see also Loki and the Builder, page 82, and Of Apples and Nuptials, page 102).

Ud: Another name for Odin.

Ulfhednar (singular Ulfhedinn): Berserkir warriors who wore wolfskins in battle, essentially becoming werewolves. Sigmund, Sigurd's father, lived for a time in the woods with his first son; they wore wolfskins, took on wolflike characteristics, and communicated by howling.

Ull: The son of Sif and the stepson of Thor. He was the god of archery and skiing, and no one was better at either. He was also renowned for his hunting skills and his ability to use a shield. Warriors prayed to him before entering a duel. Ull lived in a hall at Ydal in Asgard.

Unn: "Wave," one of the daughters of Aegir and Ran.

Urd: "Fate" or "The Past," one of the three chief norns (goddesses of fate).

Urd's Well: The well or pool where the three norns gathered to spin the fates of gods and humans. The Aesir also held a daily assembly at Urd's Well, traveling over the Bifrost bridge to get there. The well was in heaven, under the world-ash Yggdrasil and near the norns' beautiful hall. The norns poured well water and mud over Yggdrasil's roots to protect and strengthen the tree. Anything submerged in the water turned as white as the inside of an eggshell. In the well lived a pair of swans, the ancestors of all the swans on the earth.

Utgard: A fortress of the giants in Jotunheim, ruled over by Utgarda-Loki (see Thor's Journey to Utgard, page 128).

Utgarda-Loki: A clever giant skilled in magic, and a master of illusion. When Thor, Loki, and Thjalfi were on a journey,

Utgarda-Loki met them and gave them a false name, Skrymir. He used magic to make them (especially Thor) feel small and weak, pitting them against impossible opponents in contests they could never win. In the end, Utgarda-Loki revealed his trickery and admitted that he never would have believed Thor could perform as well as he did. Thor was furious, but Utgarda-Loki and his fortress disappeared before the god could take his vengeance (see Thor's Journey to Utgard, page 128).

Vafthrudnir: "Strong in Entangling (with questions)," a giant Odin once visited to test his knowledge. They engaged in a question-and-answer game, with Odin emerging the victor and Vafthrudnir losing his head.

Vafud: "Wayfarer," another name for Odin.

Vak: "Wakeful," another name for Odin.

Valaskjalf: One of Odin's halls, roofed in pure silver, where he had his all-seeing throne, Hlidskjalf (see Loki and the Builder, page 82, and Frey's Courtship, page 124).

Valgrind: The gate of Odin's hall Valhalla in Asgard.

Valhalla: "Hall of the Slain," the main hall where Odin placed his half of those killed on the battlefield. (Some were in the goddesses' temple Vingolf, and Freyja settled her share of the dead in Sessrumnir, her hall in Folkvang.) Odin's chosen warriors were known as einherjar, and in Valhalla he provided them with plenty of mead and meat (see Saehrimnir and Heidrun) when they weren't outside fighting each other for sport. Instead of fire, glowing swords provided illumination for their feasts. Valhalla was said to have 540 doorways, each big enough to allow 800 einherjar to pass through at once (see Thor and the Clay Giant, page 151, and The Doom of the Gods, page 162).

Valkyrjur, valkyries (singular valkyrja, valkyrie): "Choosers of the Slain," divine shield-maidens who accompanied Odin to battlefields. They marked those chosen to die in combat with their spears, then escorted them to Valhalla. They also provided companionship to these fallen einherjar, serving them the ever-flowing mead provided by the goat Heidrun.

Vali: (1) The son of Odin and the giantess Rind. He was born to avenge the death of Baldr, since the gods were prohibited from killing one of their own (see The Death of Baldr, page 155). Vali killed Hod when he was only one night old. It was said that he would survive Ragnarok and return with Vidar to Idavoll in Asgard (see The Doom of the Gods, page 162). (2) The son of Loki. When the gods punished Loki for Baldr's death, they turned Vali into a wolf and had him tear his brother Nari to pieces.

Van: (1) Singular of Vanir. (2) "Hope," a river formed by the flow of drool from the mouth of the wolf Fenrir (see Loki's Dangerous Children, page 86).

Vanargand: Another name for the wolf Fenrir.

Vanir (singular Van): A race of gods distinct from and thought to be older than the Aesir. After the war between these two groups at the beginning of time, they declared a truce, exchanged hostages, and intermingled on friendlier terms (see Loki and the Builder, page 82, and Loki's Head Wager, page 90). After a time, three of the Vanir—Njord, Frey, and

Freyja—were accepted as brothers and sisters of the gods of Asgard. The Vanir were also closely associated with the Ljosalfar, the light-elves.

Var: One of the Asynjur goddesses. She listened to all the oaths and agreements that people made, even in private, and punished those who broke their word.

Ve: One of the brothers of Odin. According to storyteller Snorri Sturluson, it was Ve who gave the first humans their faces, speech, hearing, and sight (see The Origin of the Cosmos and the Coming of the Gods, page 76).

Vedrfolnir: A hawk that sat between the eyes of the eagle perched at the very top of Yggdrasil.

Vegtam: "Wayfarer," another name for Odin.

Verdandi: "The Present," one of the three main norns (goddesses of fate).

Vestri: "Westerly," one of the four dwarfs that held up the giant Ymir's skull to be the sky (see The Origin of the Cosmos and the Coming of the Gods, page 76).

Vid: One of the poisonous, icy rivers known as the Elivagar that flowed out of the spring of Hvergelmir in Niflheim.

Vidar: The son of Odin and the giantess Grid. Known as the Silent God, he was nearly as strong as Thor. He lived in the green woods of Vidi in heaven and wore a thick shoe made from the scraps discarded in the making of all shoes since the world began. This shoe would help him avenge his father at Ragnarok, when he stamped on Fenrir's lower jaw and split his mouth in two before he hacked out the wolf's heart. Vidar would survive the battle and the burning of the world and return to Idavoll in Asgard along with Vali, Modi, Magni, Baldr, and Hod (see Of Apples and Nuptials, page 102, and The Doom of the Gods, page 162).

Vidblain: A third heaven, above Asgard and Andlang, where the beautiful hall Gimle was said to be. Only inhabited by Ljosalfar (light-elves) before Ragnarok, it would be a refuge for a select few afterward.

Vidi: The heavenly realm of Odin's son Vidar, a paradise of green woods and tall grasses.

Vidur: Another name for Odin.

Vidrir: Possibly "Lord of the Weather," another name for Odin.

Vigrid: The battlefield destined to be the site of Ragnarok, where the gods of Asgard would face off against the frost-giants, the fire-giants, and the hordes of Hel. The battlefield was said to measure 100 leagues (300 miles) on each side (see The Doom of the Gods, page 162).

Vili: One of the brothers of Odin. As Snorri Sturluson tells it, Vili gave consciousness and movement to the first human beings (see The Origin of the Cosmos and the Coming of the Gods, page 76).

Vingnir: (1) Thor's foster father. (2) Another name for Thor.

Vingolf: "Friend-Hall" or "Wine-Hall," a beautiful building within Asgard that was a sanctuary belonging to the goddesses.

This was where some of the einherjar chosen by Odin would be sent in the afterlife.

Volsung: A legendary king of Hunland and the father of Sigmund (see Otter's Ransom, Sigurd, and the Cursed Treasure, page 109).

Volva: The name for a seeress or wise-woman who kept stores of knowledge about the past and could foretell the future. There were many tales and poems about heroes and gods seeking out such women for their aid and wisdom.

Vor: One of the Asynjur goddesses. She was wise and curious, and nothing could be hidden from her.

Ydal: The location of Ull's high-timbered hall in Asgard.

Ygg: "Terrifier," another name for Odin.

Yggdrasil: The world-ash. Its trunk was the center of the universe, with foliage high in the heavens and roots set down in Asgard, Jotunheim, and Niflheim. A symbol of cosmic order, it was always under threat: by stags nibbling at its branches above and by the serpent Nidhogg gnawing at its roots below. Only the norns looked to preserve it, pouring healing water and mud over its root near Urd's Well. Yggdrasil got its name ("Odin's Horse") because Odin "rode" it for nine days—hanging himself from the tree in order to learn the secrets of rune magic through agony and self-sacrifice (see The Origin of the Cosmos and the Coming of the Gods, page 76, and The Doom of the Gods, page 162).

Ylg: One of the poisonous, icy rivers known as the Elivagar that flowed out of the spring of Hvergelmir in Niflheim.

Ymir: The primeval giant, born in Ginnungagap from the frosts of Niflheim being melted by the fires of Muspelheim. The milk of the cow Audhumla was his only nourishment. The sweat of his armpits produced the first frost-giants—a male and a female—and his legs mated to produce a son. Ymir was killed by the gods Odin, Vili, and Ve, and his blood drowned all the frost-giants except for Bergelmir and his wife. Then the gods used Ymir's corpse to create the world: His flesh became the land; his blood, the seas; his bones, the rocks; his skull, the sky; and his brains, the clouds. Ymir's eyelashes were set up as the ramparts of Midgard. His descendants, the frost-giants, knew Ymir as Aurgelmir (see The Origin of the Cosmos and the Coming of the Gods, page 76).

Yng, Yngvi: Other names for the god Frey. The Ynglings, royal lines in both Sweden and Norway, were said to be his descendants. Sometimes the name was written as Yngvi-Frey (see Norway, page 63).

Yrsa: The mother of King Hrolf Kraki. She later married King Adils of Sweden and gave her son what help she could when Adils plotted to kill him and his champions. She sent troops to avenge Hrolf after his death at the hands of his half-sister Skuld's army (see Bodvar Bjarki and the Champions of King Hrolf Kraki, page 137).

A GOOD START, BUT WHERE TO NOW?

I hope you've enjoyed this first step into the world of the ancient Norse—but it's only a first step. Even more tales of brave heroes and kings, bloodthirsty raiders, and daring explorers are available to anyone looking for more adventure. And you can bet that you'll find references to these mythical characters in plenty of your favorite books and movies.

If you'd like to dig further into Norse mythology, be sure to take a look at my primary sources: the *Poetic Edda* and the *Prose Edda* of the Icelandic poet-historian Snorri Sturluson. You can find many editions of both these works available for free on the internet—just be aware that these were translated 100 years ago or more, and the language can be pretty dense and archaic. Look for newer translations at your library.

If you prefer stories of heroes and kings, there are dozens of those in the sagas recorded by the Icelanders back in the thirteenth and fourteenth centuries. Snorri's collection called *Heimskringla* contains biographies of the early Norwegian kings that are fantastic—literally, in a lot of cases. There are many, many more accounts of Norse myths and history out there, including a great work by the Danish historian Saxo Grammaticus (c. 1150–1220). The 16 volumes of his *Gesta Danorum—The Danish History*—cover the story of Denmark from prehistory to the late-twelfth century.

If you'd just like to know more about how ordinary Norse people lived, the Family Sagas are a great source of information about the inner workings of life in Iceland from the Viking Age through the medieval period, and can be found in any library. A ton of scholarly work has been done examining these and the unique society that produced them. And finally, archaeologists are continuously at work all over Scandinavia and wherever the Norse peoples settled, and almost every day sheds new light on the Viking Age. Keeping up with these developments is only a website or two away. Some good ones are:

viking-archaeology-blog.blogspot.com

www.archaeology.org

www.sci-news.com/archaeology

www.smithsonianmag.com

Whether you originally thought of the Norse people as violent raiders, brave explorers, or simple farmers, you know now that they were actually all of those things. Luckily for us, they were also gifted poets and storytellers. Their myths and sagas will continue to fascinate us and inspire our imaginations as long as there are people like you eager to seek out knowledge. Unlike Odin, you won't even have to give up an eye.

* * *

Family Trees of the Gods

Aesir

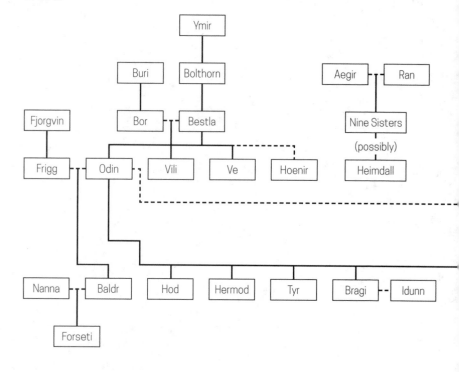

Vanir and Loki

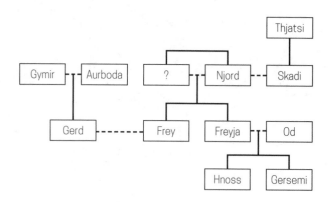

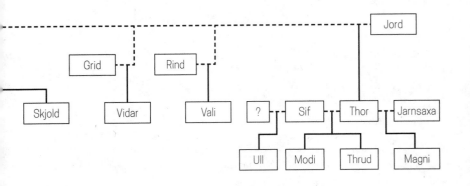

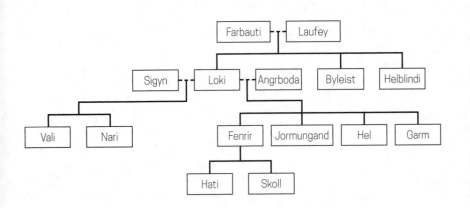

Other Ulysses Press Books

INTRODUCTION TO GREEK MYTHOLOGY FOR KIDS
Richard Marcus, Natalie Buczynsky, and Jonathan Shelnutt
$14.95

Take a journey through Mount Olympus, ancient Greece, and ancient Rome with this collection of the greatest tales found in Greek and Roman mythology. From origin stories to family drama, you'll learn about the most powerful Olympic gods, including Zeus, Hera, Poseidon, Athena, Apollo, Artemis, Aphrodite, Hades, and more.

THE UNOFFICIAL HOGWARTS COOKBOOK FOR KIDS
Alana Al-Hatlani
$17.95

Calling all Potterheads! It's time to whip up something spellbinding in the kitchen. With 50 easy-to-follow, low-mess recipes, you and your kids will learn to cook all of the best wizarding world favorites.

FUN AND FRIENDLY CALLIGRAPHY FOR KIDS
Virginia Lucas Hart
$15.95

The art of calligraphy doesn't teach you how to write words, but instead, how to draw them. With this book's fun and playful approach, you will not only improve your handwriting skills, you'll have an absolute blast while doing so!

WWII BATTLE TRIVIA FOR KIDS
Brette Sember
$14.95
Learn about what life was like on the battlefield, the first battle fought, blitzkriegs, submarines, and so much more! Written in question-and-answer format, this book is perfect for reluctant readers or any kid who just loves history.

DRAWING DRAGONS
Sandra Staple
$16.95
In easy-to-follow, step-by-step detail, *Drawing Dragons* teaches you all the tricks and techniques you'll need to create your own amazing dragons. You'll discover how to draw all types of dragons using nothing but a pencil.

To order these books, call 800-377-2542 or 510-601-8301, fax 510-601-8307, e-mail ulysses@ulyssespress.com, or write to Ulysses Press, P.O. Box 3440, Berkeley, CA 94703. All retail orders are shipped free of charge. California residents must include sales tax. Allow two to three weeks for delivery.

About the Author

Peter Aperlo has written for the rather disparate realms of academic archaeology, pen-and-paper role-playing games, "Making of..." film books, video games, and screenplays for TV and feature films. This book takes him back to his days as a graduate student and summers spent digging in Denmark, with its pickled herring and horizontal rain. He lives in California with his wife and two daughters.